MY COMPREHENSION HUB

OBJECTIVE, SUBJECTIVE AND PERSONAL RESPONSE QUESTIONS, VOCABULARY AND GRAMMAR ACTIVITIES, EXPLANATION OF GRAMMAR CONCEPTS & SOLVED ANSWERS

FIROZ TATA

ISBN 979-888546452-9

For the first time to my dear readers,

Back then, as a child, I was destined to encounter numerous terrible experiences with my several teachers. As a kid, I had my share of horrible experiences at home too that no child deserves. However, even if I want to dedicate any of my books to any of my teachers, I can't. It's heartbreaking, isn't it?

After miserably failing in English in the last and decisive year of my schooling, no one but only me through the burning desire, dedication and determination in my heart knew that one day I would become a published author. Years later, I successfully did.

Therefore, I sincerely want to dedicate this book to all the students who are struggling now and have less confidence with the English language, yet determined to practice and gradually improve.

I dedicate this book to all those students who mistakenly think that their English can never improve.

I also dedicate this book to my resolve of never quitting on the path of enriching myself with knowledge and improving with the passing years.

Contents

Preface

My Dear Readers,

Although the preface is the first part of the book that one reads, it is the last part that I created. After nearly a month of writing, editing and finalizing the matter, I have come up with my sixth and final title (book) of the year 2021. With the grace of Lord Ahura Mazda and my unconditional love for some precious people in my heart, it was yet another splendid year of my writing profession. Although for more than thirteen years I have loved writing for my zealous readers, sometimes creating a manuscript can end in extreme physical and mental exhaustion. However, I take such experiences as the choice of my peace and pleasure.

Besides being one of the significant subjects in the curriculum, English is also the medium through which various other subjects are taught. A good practice and command over English always helps the students to study their other subjects with confidence and convenience. Nonetheless, this is my opportunity of enormous ecstasy to present to you on the auspicious day of Christmas my yet another title 'My Comprehension Hub'. This book not only intends to drastically improve the reading skills of the students but will also assist to practice their English in a much better and confident manner.

Reading a comprehension passage is the ability to process the given text and understand its exact meaning. Therefore, My Comprehension Hub will serve as a certain need to practice and learn the engrossing language of English in various grades of secondary schools. The book will also assist those who desire to improve their understanding, reading, writing and grammatical expertise. I have made my best attempt to choose informative as well as captivating topics followed by related objective and subjective questions as well as grammar activities. Wherever necessary, for further clarification and knowledge, I have added easy explanations of important grammar concepts. By solving English Question Quarters followed after every passage, students will find themselves deeply engrossed and connected to the language. Besides, inclusion of the answer section at the end of the book will make the learning more stress-free and assured.

I am confident that this book will nurture and enrich the fondness of the users, helping them to accomplish their set goals in English. The students are bound to exceed the general standards of achievement. A thorough study and practice of the given passages will prove to be very useful for students expanding their horizons of language understanding. It will also help them to appear in the examination with more confidence. I have no doubt that this book will be equally accepted, applauded and appreciated by principals, parents, teachers and their students.

I sincerely expect that My Comprehension Hub will help the teachers with immense pleasure and pride to teach their dear pupils to practice and prepare themselves from examination point of view and make the subject matter more informative and attention grabbing. Furthermore, as always, I have tried my level best to use student-friendly, intelligible and lucid language throughout the book. Let me assure you that this publication will not only go a very long way in serving the students to be good English learners but will also assist them to discover several thought-provoking facts through the covered topics.

Kindly share your valuable reviews of the book on... ***reviewmypublications@gmail.com***

– The Author

Acknowledgements

As I always acknowledge in each of my books,

From deep down my heart, I would love to express my earnest care and gratefulness to my beloved mother Ms. Heera Tata to always be my supporter no matter what. Each time she has raised my spirit and unconditionally encouraged me during my ups and downs in my writing journeys.

Not to forget acknowledging my kind-hearted, selfless, sharp-minded, extremely supportive, very caring and beautiful poet-sister Ms. Harshada (Zenith), to help me with her editing skills and extremely valuable suggestions wherever necessary for the betterment of the book. For more than two decades I keep thanking my lucky stars to have her as my *rakhi* sister.

I would also like to extend my heartfelt gratitude to Notion Press publishers for providing an outstanding platform of Xpress Publishing, helping me to author my 19th title (book) for them.

Lastly, I also want to thank every single one of you who appreciates my writings and who says, “You have to use My Comprehension Hub” to their family members, dear friends and relatives.

– The Author

ONE

TIME AND PRIORITIES

Having a lack of time to do things is the most troublesome complaint that almost everybody has. Initially, time management was considered something related to busy people only. Nowadays, almost everyone falls under the same category of shortage of time. With dedication and discipline, personal as well as professional life can be well organized once a person learns to manage his/her time efficiently. It further not only benefits one's mental and physical health but also provides a sense of control and satisfaction in life. People who work in accord with their time tend to lead much happier, gratified and affluent lives.

The techniques of time management are not fixed or rigid. One has to look for the practices that best suit them for a productive and optimum outcome. In some way or the other, we all tend to practice time management. One must take care of how maturely the effectiveness of our methods is maximized.

Setting clear-minded goals is essential. This means that whenever we set out to do something, we should be fully aware about the purpose we have to accomplish. This would not only give us a sense of direction but also would help us to allot specific time to whatever tasks we have to fulfil. Moreover, setting clear priorities in our mind is significant. We should be fully aware of the fact that what is more important to us, and things that require our instant attention. Prioritizing would help us to assess our abilities, needs and necessities in the long term. Thus, the ultimate doorway to success opens after we start to prioritize things in life. While prioritizing, a person should be aware of those aspects of time that are not contributing to the long term set goals.

Many people prefer to keep a diary to plan their day-to-day activities. Several online planners, digital applications and software are available so that one can access routine plans from home or from work. However, using the conventional diary is better as it lets us get off the screen for some time and think of our priorities with a peaceful mind. To conclude, time management and prioritizing is surely a more satisfying way to lead a successful life. They further help in controlling what we do to reduce our stress while improving health.

English Question Quarters

(A) State whether the following statements are true or false:

(1) People do not complain about having a lack of time.
(2) We must maximize the effectiveness of our time management methods.
(3) It is not that vital to stay clear minded while setting our goals.
(4) Success depends on how well a person prioritizes things in life.

(B) Based on the passage complete the following:

(1) Keep a....
(2) Prioritizing helps....
(3) Practice....
(4) Time management and prioritizing reduces....

(C) Activities based on vocabulary:

(1) Pick out any five compound words from the passage.

(2) Using the given prefixes (im, mis, un, in, dis) make antonyms for the given words.
(a) management (b) ability (c) maturely (d) professional

(D) Activities based on grammar:

(1) Many people prefer to keep a diary to plan their day-to-day activities.
(Rewrite the sentence without changing its meaning. Begin with, Only a few ....)

(2) Several online planners, digital applications and software are available.
(Rewrite as a rhetorical question)

(3) The ultimate doorway to success opens after we start to prioritize things in life.
(Use 'when' and rewrite the sentence)

(4) The techniques of managing time are fixed or rigid.
(Rewrite the correct sentence by rectifying the error)

(E) Answer the following personal response questions:
(1) "Time once lost, is lost forever." Do you agree with this? Justify.
(2) Do you think that prioritizing things in life is helpful? In what way?
(3) Should a person keep a diary to plan day-to-day activities? Give your opinion.
(4) "Your time is limited, so don't waste it living someone else's life." What are your views about this statement?

(F) Read and understand the above passage well to write a short summary on it. Suggest a suitable title. *(In the summary, only the main points from the passage are to be written. Details and examples are to be avoided.)*

TWO

SUMO

Sports and sports-related activities are extremely popular in Japan. Sumo is a 2000-year-old form of wrestling. Many regard it to be the national sport of Japan. In the early Edo period (1603 – 1868), sumo emerged as a professional sport. Although amateur wrestlers practice it, it has its greatest appeal as a professional spectator sport. Almost every month, tournaments lasting for 15 days take place.

The main objective of this sport is for a wrestler to force his opponent out of the *dohyo*, which is the center circle of the elevated cement-hard clay ring. In other words, force the opponent to touch the surface of the *dohyo* with any part of his body other than the soles of his feet. Sometimes, the actual conflict is only a matter of a few seconds. In order to determine who has stepped out or touched down first is often extremely difficult. It requires the closest attention of a referee who is dressed in the court outfit of 14th century noblemen. The judges sit around the *dohyo* at floor level.

The JSA (Japan Sumo Association) has officially listed 82 winning techniques consisting of assorted lifts, shoves, throws, trips and pulls. Almost 48 of them are regarded as the 'classic' techniques. However, distinctive to sumo is the use of a bellyband or belt called a *mawashi*. In most of the sumo matches wrestlers face a firm challenge from their opponents. Two-handed grip on the opponent's *mawashi* while blocking him from getting a similar grip on his is widely practiced in the sport. Professional sumo wrestlers are ranked in a pyramid, rising from the beginners at the bottom to grand champions called '*yokozuna*' in the sport at the top.

English Question Quarters

(A) Choose the correct option from the following:

(1) The center circle of the sumo ring is called ...
(a) *yokozuna*
(b) *mawashi*
(c) *dohyo*

(2) Sumo is practiced by ...
(a) the common people of Japan
(b) amateur wrestlers
(c) grand champions called 'yokozuna'

(3) Professional sumo wrestlers are ranked on the bases of ...
(a) a pyramid
(b) matches
(c) Japan Sumo Association

(B) Complete the following and answer the given questions:

(1) Sumo is a 2000-year-old form of wrestling that is regarded by many to be ...
(2) It is extremely difficult to ...
(3) What is the main object of the sumo sport?
(4) Write on the officially listed 82 winning techniques of the sport.
(5) What is distinctive to sumo? Explain its use.

(C) Activities based on vocabulary:

(1) Pick out words from the passage referring to...
(a) A person you are playing or fighting against in a game or sport.
(b) A person engaged in a sporting activity as a pastime rather than professionally.
(c) To make something happen in a particular way or type.

(2) Choose the correct connotation of the given words in context of the passage.

(a) Tournaments
(i) two-handed grip on the opponent (ii) sumo wrestling (iii) sports contests

(b) Noblemen
(i) who used to go on wars (ii) did wrestle (iii) referees dressed like them

(D) Activities based on grammar:

(1) Make two sentences of your choice by using the word 'face' as a noun as well as a verb.

(2) Change and rewrite the Degree of Comparison as directed without altering the meaning.
(a) According to me, Hakuhō Shō is the greatest of all wrestlers. (Positive)
(b) Hakuhō Shō is one of the most talented of all wrestlers. (Comparative)
(c) No one in the sumo tournament is as brilliant as Hakuhō Shō. (Superlative)

(3) Choose the appropriate adverb or adjective form to fill in the blanks.
(a) He was very ________ to see the wrestling match. (excitedly / excited)
(b) He would become a ________ wrestler one day. (great / greatly)
(c) The heavy wrestler walked very ________. (slow / slowly)

(4) We have a dozen experienced coaches and several strong sumo wrestlers to participate in the competition.
(Rewrite the sentence using 'as well as...')

(E) Answer the following personal response questions:
(1) Describe a sumo-wrestling match that you may have seen on television.
(2) Which game/sport do you like the most and enjoy playing? Describe what you know about it?
(3) There are various types/forms of wrestling. Do you have any favourite wrestler whose feats have impressed you a lot? Provide a short essay type information on any one of them.

(F) Read and understand the above passage well to write a short summary on it. Suggest a suitable title.

THREE

Flora Saves Herself

Flora was a beautiful young girl who was an orphan. She lived alone. One day along with her friends, she went to fetch some fresh water from the nearby brook.

One of the friends said, "My father is getting me married to the richest boy in the village."

The second friend said, "My elder brother has collected bags of gold and money to spend it on my wedding."

The third one could not keep herself quiet so she too said, "My parents will make me marry the knight of our kingdom."

One of the girls asked sarcastically, "Flora, what are your plans for marriage, or aren't you ever going to get married!" Flora replied. "Although I am an orphan, I do have a wealthy aunt living in the town. She will bring me rich clothes, sweets, money and jewellery, placing everything on a golden platter on the day I get married."

At the same time, a rogue was passing by who overheard their conversation. Instantly he was attracted to Flora's beauty. He decided to marry her. Next day he disguised himself as a jeweller and visited to her hut. Placing on a golden platter, he carried with him rich clothes, sweets, money and jewellery.

The rogue knocked the door and gorgeous Flora opened it to see a stranger standing in front of her. "I am your uncle from the town. At the time of your parents' death, I had promised them to make you marry a very rich boy. I have found the right groom for you. Get ready at once, we are leaving for the town right away," said the rogue.

The girl was astonished to hear all this and before she could think anything, the cad insisted, "Be fast, we have to reach the town before the nightfall." Flora quickly collected all her necessary stuff and left with him. The cunning man took the girl to his wrecked house in the woods. On reaching, he revealed the truth that he was not her uncle and he wanted to marry her. Poor Flora began to cry. She opposed and kept crying, but her tears had no effect on the scoundrel. Soon he left the girl with his old mother and went out for marriage arrangements.

"How do you manage such long hair?" the old woman questioned. Flora artfully replied, "I keep my head in a mortar and then caress it with a pestle!" Without wasting any time, the silly old woman put her head into the mortar and asked the girl to caress it with a pestle. Flora immediately hit the pestle on her head. The old woman fainted. Smart Flora dressed her with a bridal costume and made her sit on a chair with a covered face. Finally, Flora fled from the crook's house and saved herself.

English Question Quarters

(A) Read the passage carefully and solve the following activities:

(1) Pick out the false sentences and write them correctly:

(a) The three friends went to fetch some fresh water from the nearby brook.

(b) Flora succeeded in escaping from the rogue's house to save herself.

(c) The rogue said that he was her uncle from the town.

(d) Flora opposed and kept screaming, but it did not affect the old woman.

(2) Who said the following words to whom?
(a) My parents will make me marry the knight of our kingdom.
(b) Be fast, we have to reach the town before the sun sets.
(c) How do you manage such long hair?
(d) My father is getting me married to the richest boy in the village.
(e) My elder brother has collected bags of gold and money to spend it on my wedding.
(f) I am your uncle from the town.
(g) Although I am an orphan, I do have a wealthy aunt living in the town.

(B) Answer the following questions in one or in a few sentences:
(1) Where did Flora and her friends go?
(2) What reply did Flora give to her friends? Answer in your own words.
(3) What did the rogue carry with him to Flora's hut?
(4) In your own words, narrate conservation between Flora and the old woman.
(5) Describe the old woman in one word from the passage.

(C) Activities based on vocabulary:
(1) Pick up as many words as possible from the passage related to Flora.
(2) Pick up as many words as possible from the passage related to the person who visited Flora.

(D) Activities based on grammar:

(1) Although she had never seen him, she left with him.
(Rewrite using 'but' as a coordinator)

(2) She will bring rich clothes, sweets, money and jewellery.
(Frame 'Wh-' question to get the underlined part as the answer)

(3) The rogue was attracted to Flora, but he could not marry her.
(Rewrite beginning with 'Though...')

(4) "How do you manage such long hair?" questioned the old woman.
(Rewrite in indirect speech)

(5) flora opened it to see a stranger standing in front of her i am your uncle from the town
(Punctuate the sentence correctly)

(E) Answer the following personal response questions:
(1) What would you do if someone forces you for a marriage against your wish?
(2) What reply would you have given to your friends if you were in the place of Flora?
(3) On the basis of your imagination, what can happen further in the story with Flora after she escapes from the rogue's house?

(F) Read and understand the above passage well to write a short summary on it. Suggest a suitable title.

FOUR
EDUCATION

Education is regarded as one of the fundamental values on which one's success highly depends. To understand the role of education in attaining success, one has to understand first how it influences a successful life. Person's wealth, fame, career, assets and most of all, personality, can claim a successful life. People think that those born with wealth are already successful. However, the truth is that being born with assets will not make us a successful person until we prove ourselves to be worthy of it.

Why do people lay more emphasis on being educated in order to be successful? Well, it is quite simple. Education gives us the sense of direction, knowledge, skills and focus which is needed in order to be successful. Moreover, a good foundation is also important, as many who have succeeded in their career have done so because they took correct decisions at the correct time. Our decision-making abilities heavily depend on our education and level of experience.Moreover, education makes us stand out among the others, gives us an edge, self-respect and elegance. The chances of having a better-paid job and even a better career heavily depend on the education we attain.

We cannot just sit down and keep dreaming. The best thing to do is take charge of self and perceive education. Educational degrees would not only land us in better paying jobs, but also make us worthy of it. Our personality and values would be shaped by the education we get, which would help us to deal with occupational and business situations that otherwise leave us disordered. Therefore, let's walk together in the direction of a good education. Education is the key to success as it transforms our knowledge, values and outlook towards the path to success. Let us create education for all.

English Question Quarters

(A) Fill in the blanks with the correct alternatives:

(1) Our __________ abilities heavily depend on our education and level of experience. (dreaming / decision-making)

(2) Education influences a __________ life. (successful / professional)

(3) __________ is regarded as one of the fundamental values. (success / education)

(4) People think that those who are born with __________ are already successful. (wealth / power)

(B) Answer the following questions in one or in a few sentences:

(1) How can one claim a successful life?

(2) What does education give us?

(3) Why is good education regarded as the key to success?

(C) Activities based on vocabulary:

(1) Match the words in line (a) with their meanings in line (b).

(a) (i) elegance (ii) attain (iii) edge (iv) experience (v) fundamental

(b) (i) the most important and central part of something (ii) on the verge (iii) successful path (iv) attractive and showing a good sense of style (v) a skill or a knowledge gained doing something after a period of time (vi) accomplish

(2) By using the following words, create sentences of your choice.
(a) self-respect (b) focus (c) career (d) business (e) perceive

(D) Activities based on grammar:

(1) Rewrite the sentences by choosing correct question tags given in the brackets below.
(isn't it?, wasn't it?, don't they?, will it?, can we?)

(a) Wealth, fame, career, assets and personality claims success.
(b) A good education is the key to success.
(c) We cannot just sit down and keep dreaming.
(d) Being born with assets will not make us a successful person.

(2) Make suitable changes wherever necessary and rewrite the sentences using 'not only.... but also....'

(a) Education gives us the sense of direction, knowledge, skills and focus to succeed.
(b) Education makes us stand out among the others, gives us an edge, self-respect and elegance.

(3) Find two sentences from the above passage that contain infinitives. ***(Note: The infinitives without 'to' before them are called, 'bare infinitives'.)***

(4) Let us create education for all.
(Begin the sentence with 'Let education ...' and rewrite)

(E) Answer the following personal response questions:
(1) Write about the different problems that children in our society face keeping them away from educating themselves.
(2) Mention some of the efforts that you can make to spread education among underprivileged children around you.
(3) According to you, is education important for a good life? Explain.

(F) Read and understand the above passage well to write a short summary on it. Suggest a suitable title.

FIVE

PLASTIC AND ENVIRONMENT

Plastic bags are one of the most dangerous things used on our planet. It causes harm in several ways to the environment. At times, we presume that plastic bags cannot do so much harm, but they adversely contribute to our environment in several ways. Use of plastic bags litter the surroundings. Rivers, lakes, seas, oceans and forests are polluted in different parts of the world as winds carry these bags everywhere. Most of us do not even realize the hazardous consequences of using plastic bags. One of the researches shows that every year people in America use over a billion such bags.

Plastic bags can even kill wildlife. They not only kill aquatic animals, but also terrestrial animals. Many species are already in danger of extinction. About one million mammals and seabirds die every year by swallowing plastic bags. Plastic is mistaken as food by them and gradual choking leads to their slow and painful death. Research shows that every year nearly a lakh of marine mammals die due to this.

Polyethylene, which is a type of petroleum, is a substance used to make plastic bags. Petroleum is a mineral oil that is found under the ground or the sea. It is used to produce petrol, paraffin, diesel, oil, gas, etc. Petroleum is a major source of energy that helps in generating electricity, heat and light. As tons of plastic bags are manufactured each year, tons of petroleum are wasted in manufacturing them. Polyethylene is not only bad for our environment but also can be potentially toxic for human survival.

Burning plastic is a global problem as it emits toxic gases that harm the atmosphere and increase the level of Volatile Organic Compounds in the air. These compounds are organic chemicals that have a high vapour pressure at ordinary room temperature. Plastic bags are non-biodegradable as it takes more than a thousand years to breakdown. Burning these bags does not help either, as they cause air pollution. When such bags are burned, toxic fumes are released into the air as well as soil.

Tons of plastic debris from large containers are discarded every year. It is very evident that this pollutes lands, rivers, shorelines, beaches and oceans. Plastic is one of the deadly inventions of man. Over the last few years, there has been a massive increase in plastic packaging for various items, having a major negative impact on humanity, animals and environment. We only have one world to live in, so more consciousness is required in taking care of it.

English Question Quarters

(A) The teacher will write a few incomplete sentences on the board and will ask the students to complete them in their own words:

(1) According to the passage, petroleum is wasted because...

(2) The writer in the passage encourages us to...

(3) The deadly results of using plastic bags are...

(4) Today, I have decided that I will never use plastic bags because...

(B) Answer the following questions in one or in a few sentences:

(1) Explain the role of winds in context to plastic bags.

(2) Wildlife is killed due to plastic bags. Explain.
(3) What is petroleum? In what it is used?
(4) Why is burning plastic a global problem? What are its hazards?

(C) Activities based on vocabulary:

(1) Spot out another word for 'world' used in the passage.

(2) Make a list of as many words as possible from the passage that indicates nature.

(3) Write the names of any five aquatic animals.

(4) Write the names of any five terrestrial animals.

(5) The following compound words from the passage are spelt in jumbled order. Rearrange the letters to make them meaningful.
(a) e f l i d w l i ____________ (b) g a g n i c k p a ____________ (c) t a e h ____________ (d) o k d w n e a b r ____________

(D) Activities based on grammar:

(1) Plastic bags are one of the most dangerous things used on our planet.
(Rewrite using the subject pronoun 'we')

(2) About one million mammals and seabirds die every year.
(Rewrite beginning with the underline part)

(3) It is very evident.
(Rewrite as an exclamatory sentence)

(4) Wildlife has been facing deaths.
(Name the tense of the underlined verb)

(5) Environmentalists advised us.
(Rewrite in the Past Perfect Continuous Tense)

(E) Answer the following personal response questions:
(1) Can you absolutely stop the use of plastic bags in your everyday life? What steps would you take? Suggest some of your other actions to limit the impact of plastic bags.
(2) How would you feel and react if you personally come across an animal suffering due to the consumption of a plastic bag? Will you try to save its life? How?
(3) Write some of the recommendations suggested in terms of the problems associated with plastic bags.

(F) Read and understand the above passage well to write a short summary on it. Suggest a suitable title.

SIX

CHOLESTEROL

In 1812, cholesterol was first discovered. Its name originates from the Greek word 'cholestereos-oi', meaning 'bile-solid'. Cholesterol is a fatty substance found in the blood, fat and most of the tissues in the human body. In other words, it is a waxy, fat-like substance found in all the cells in our body. It is an organic compound existing either in a free state or as esters of fatty acid in almost all animal tissues. Cholesterol is also used by the human body for the digestive system. The creation of this compound takes place in different tissues and organs especially, the brain, liver and arteries.

Increase of cholesterol in the human body above a certain level can prove to be hazardous for one's health. The free flow of the blood is obstructed when excessive fat and cholesterol are deposited on the walls of the arteries. This causes blockage of blood flow resulting in heart problems. The amount of blood flowing in the arteries decreases and as a result, the oxygen supply to important parts of our body decreases. Thus, small blood clots passing through the blood vessels are trapped due to the higher amount of cholesterol deposits. Some of the important warning signs of high cholesterol include shortness of breath, numbness, nausea, slurred speech, chest pain or angina, extreme fatigue, extreme coldness and high blood pressure.

If arteries providing oxygen and carrying blood to the heart are blocked, then that particular part of the heart stops its normal functioning. This immediately leads to a major heart attack that can even prove fatal. However, we can control the level of cholesterol in our blood through the correct diet. A high percentage of cholesterol is present in the foods of animal origin like meat, eggs, butter, ghee, cheese, etc. We must avoid foods containing more cholesterol. Fresh green leafy vegetables, fruits, cornflakes, pulses and cereals must be the major part of our every day diet.

Cholesterol is bio-synthesized by all animal cells and is essentially a structural component of animal cell membranes. Our body needs a certain amount of cholesterol to make hormones, vitamin D and substances that help in the digestion of various foods. Thus, the body makes all the cholesterol it needs. Several measures can be undertaken to maintain the desirable cholesterol level in our body. For a healthy life we must not only regularly do exercise, yoga, cycling and walking but also control the consumption of fatty foods that helps in reducing health risks.

English Question Quarters

(A) Choose the correct alternatives and complete the following sentences:

(1) As a fatty substance, cholesterol is found in ____________________

(a) human brain

(b) the blood, fat and most of the tissues

(c) hormones and vitamins

(2) As the flow of the blood in the arteries decreases ____________________

(a) the speed of digestion process increases

(b) the levels of fresh oxygen increases in the blood

(c) the supply of oxygen to important parts of our body decreases

(3) More cholesterol is present in ________________________

(a) the foods of animal origin

(b) obese individuals

(c) the blood vessels

(4) To maintain the desirable cholesterol level in blood __________________________________

(a) eat meat, eggs, butter, ghee, cheese, etc. regularly

(b) a person must start consuming certain fatty foods

(c) regular physical mobility and exercise are essential

(B) Complete the reasons and answer the given questions:

(1) Foods of animal origin like meat, eggs, butter, ghee, cheese, etc. must be avoided because ______________________

(2) Exercise, yoga, cycling, walking and control over the consumption of certain fatty foods are important because ______________________

(3) Heart problems result because ____

(4) Mention some of the important warning signs of high cholesterol.

(5) Which foods must be avoided by us? What must be the major part of our daily diet?

(6) Why does the body make all the cholesterol it needs?

(C) Activities based on vocabulary:

(1) Find out the synonyms from the passage that means...

(a) involving risk or danger _______________

(b) to obstruct something _______________

(c) to find something _______________

(d) without delay _______________

(e) completely necessary _______________

(2) Pick out the words and group of words that indicate different kinds of foodstuffs mentioned in the passage.

(3) Classify the given words in the four categories of noun, verb, adjective and adverb.
(body, essentially, animal, meat, part, healthy, functioning, small, found, decreases, obstructed, only, high, prove, fresh, hazardous, eggs, especially, regularly, consumption, immediately, include)

(D) Activities based on grammar:

(1) Fill in the blanks with appropriate articles:

(a) Blocked arteries leads to ______ major heart attack.

(b) It is ______ organic compound.

(c) ______ oxygen supply to important parts of our body should not decrease.

(d) Cholesterol is a fatty substance found in ______ blood.

(e) Human body needs ______ certain amount of cholesterol.

(2) When the patient arrived the doctor was reading his reports.
(Name and identify the subordinate clause)

(3) The doctor listened to the patient but said nothing.
(Rewrite the sentence beginning 'Though...')

(4) She fainted and fell to the ground.
(Rewrite using a present participle in place of the underlined word)

(5) The blood would not stop flowing.
(Rewrite without 'not')

(E) Answer the following personal response questions:
(1) Due to wrong lifestyle and eating habits, if your cholesterol shoots up and if your doctor warns you to keep a check on it before your health deteriorates further what steps will you take to start having a healthier and fitter life?
(2) Do you consider it easy to maintain good health? Why?
(3) What message do you wish to give to those who are careless with regard to their health?

(F) Read and understand the above passage well to write a short summary on it. Suggest a suitable title.

SEVEN

In Search of a Hope

The most risky and dangerous thing a person can do is to make negative, destructive and irreversible decisions. This damaging attitude destroys families. Such decisions are taken when he is at his lowest, weighted down by overwhelming surrounding conditions. However, he should believe in himself and soon there will be a breakthrough for the betterment. He will overcome all the obstacles and challenges and come out victorious. He will emerge from the dark by breaking through the defeats that have set him back for a very long time and say, "It was all for the best!"

The first question that probably arises in his mind is... When will a breakthrough take place? The breakthrough could occur today, tomorrow or the next day. Neither he is aware nor anyone else. Only the Almighty who has created his destiny has the answer to the question.

The second question that probably arises in his mind is... How long can he continue and hold on with such hurting circumstances? A lot longer than he thinks, he can! Most of the therapists say... "We witness our patients for several months, perhaps for a few years. Abruptly one day, through nothing precise that we could tell that we fixed, the skin that had dropped and looked pale appeared pink and healthy. The drowsy eyes that were dull get sparkled." This is a phenomenal movement because hope is a phenomenon. One fails to understand what activates a ray of hope or from where it actually originates. Therefore, when a person discovers hope, there borns a completely new individual.

One can find new hope when he realizes that today is the fresh beginning. What appears like an end never is unless we decide to bring the end. At some point or the other, there is surely a breakthrough for each one of us. This breakthrough totally depends on us. We all have self-imposed restrictions that hold us back. Most likely, a newer version of self will not occur until we power beyond our set parameters. When we start to push beyond our limits, the impossible starts to become possible.

English Question Quarters

(A) Solve the following activities:

(1) Rearrange the following in the order of occurrence in the passage. Read the passage again if you are uncertain.

(a) Neither he nor anyone else is aware when a breakthrough will take place.
(b) The drowsy and dull eyes sparkled.
(c) There is surely a breakthrough for all of us.
(d) A person should believe in himself.
(e) A lot longer than one thinks a person can continue and hold on with hurting circumstances.

(2) Fill in the blanks with the correct alternatives:

(a) ______________ is a phenomenon. (challenge / failures / hope)
(b) The drowsy eyes that were dull gets ______________. (pink / sparkled / pale)
(c) The ______________ starts to become possible. (answer / impossible /question)
(d) The ______________ totally depends on us. (breakthrough / tomorrow / today)

(e) We all have self-imposed ____________. (parameters / originates / restrictions)

(B) Answer the following questions in one or in a few sentences:

(1) What and when is the most risky and dangerous thing a person can do?
(2) Who has the answer to the first question that arises in the mind? What is the question?
(3) How long can one continue and hold the hurting circumstances?
(4) What one fails to understand? When is the completely new individual born?
(5) When will a newer version of self occur?

(C) Activities based on vocabulary:

(1) Choose the correct option that conveys the exact meaning.

(a) probably (possible / perhaps / phenomenal)
(b) originates (initiates / ignites / imagines)
(c) parameters (longings / lines / limits)
(d) phenomenon (marvel / magical / mesmerizing)

(2) Pick out as many compound words as possible from the passage.

(3) Write the noun forms of the following words coming in the passage.

(a) victorious (b) emerge (c) totally (d) healthy (e) originate

(4) Find synonyms of the following from the passage.

(a) improvement (b) triggers (c) very powerful to resist (d) sleepy (e) limitations (f) permanent

(D) Activities based on grammar:

(1) we witness our patients for several months perhaps for a few years *(Punctuate the sentence correctly)*

(2) What appears to be not the end is always the end unless we decide to bring the end.
(Spot the errors and rewrite the sentence correctly)

(3) This damaging attitude destroys families. *(Pick out the gerund)*

(4) You <u>must</u> respect what the therapist said.
(State what the underline modal auxiliary indicates) ***(Note: An Auxiliary is a helping verb and a Modal Auxiliary is a helper verb that helps the main verb express some meaning like possibility, advice, ability, obligation, etc.)***

(5) We <u>should</u> push beyond our limits to change impossible to possible.
(State what the underline modal auxiliary indicate)

(E) Answer the following personal response questions:

(1) Describe in your words the two contradictory pictures depicted in the passage.
(2) What does this passage convey to you?

(F) Read and understand the above passage well to write a short summary on it. Suggest a suitable title.

EIGHT
SAMUDRAGUPTA

Samudragupta was the greatest among all the Gupta rulers. He succeeded his father Chandragupta I. Due to his conquest in different directions, for his acts of bravery and remarkable leadership, Dr. Vincent Smith regards him as the 'Napoleon of India'. His military conquests are known from *Prayag Prashati* written by his court poet Harisena.

As Samudragupta was educated, with the passage of time he emerged as an accomplished scholar. Moreover, he fought several successful battles in his lifetime. Several scholars and historians agree that he was selected by his father as a successor due to his real worth. The decision of Samudragupta as the successor was publically announced in an open assembly and the young Samudra was asked to protect his subjects. Everyone, besides Samudragupta's brothers, were overjoyed with Chandragupta I's decision.

Samudragupta has been an inspiration for his great accomplishment. He is considered as one of the most memorable Gupta emperors whose period is distinguished as the age of fine art and learning. His all-round and multi-dimensional qualities stood apart from his contemporary Indian rulers. His razor-sharp intelligence and military qualities as a warrior displayed at its highest grade. Thus, one has to agree that he was a model ruler among other supreme kings of the time. He was a great scholar-poet who also learnt Vedas, a superb hunter and an excellent warrior. As he was an empire-builder and a political leader of higher calibre, he holds a unique spot in ancient Indian history. He did not seize the distant kingdoms, but won them over by his policy of conciliation. He was a kind of ruler who pardoned those who submitted to him. This displays that he was also a man of serious diplomatic skills as seen by the treatment he gave to all who acknowledged his authority. He showed kindness to the poor, needy and helped the distressed.

This great Gupta king was not only a great conqueror but also an outstanding diplomat. We can assume by the way he treated the ruler whom he defeated. Like a cultured man he returned the kingdom of the rulers of South India, as he was aware that it would be difficult to administer such distant territories due to lack of transport and communication amenities. He is also credited for his contribution in the advancement of Indian culture. He was known for his fondness for poetries and music, earning him the title of '*Kaviraja*'. A poetical work called '*Krishna Charitam*' is attributed to him. His lyric coins show him playing a musical instrument, veena. Harisena has described his emperor as a kind and charitable man.

The period of Samudragupta was an era of all round success. This period was followed by the much more flourishing period of Chandragupta II Vikramaditya whose period is also known as the Golden Period of ancient Indian history. However, according to many, the Golden Period actually began during the reign of Samudragupta.

English Question Quarters

(A) State whether the following statements are true or false:

(1) Samudragupta's military conquests are known from *Krishna Charitam*.

(2) Chandragupta I selected Samudragupta as his successor.

(3) Chandragupta II Vikramaditya was the father of Samudragupta.

(4) Samudragupta was a great scholar-writer of his times.

(5) Golden Period actually began during the reign of Samudragupta.

(B) Based on the passage, write on the qualities and general information of the great Gupta emperor Samudragupta with the help of clues give:
(1) Samudragupta was educated and later....
(2) The period of Samudragupta is distinguished as....
(3) At its highest grade, the emperor displayed his....
(4) In the history of ancient India, Samudragupta....
(5) He displayed compassion towards....

(C) Activities based on vocabulary:

(1) The following compound words from the passage are spelt in jumbled order. Rearrange and write the letters to make them meaningful.
(a) d h e i s u g n i t i d s ______________ (b) l a c i s u m ______________ (c) u p g t a r a d a m u s ______________
(d) e m o p r y a r n t o c ______________ (e) o g d s m i k n ______________

(2) Find and understand the usage of the following words in the passage. Write their meanings based on the text.
(a) successor (b) grade (c) kind (d) ruler (e) period

(3) Make meaningful sentences using the following group of words.
(a) passage of time (b) by the way (c) aware of the fact (d) diplomatic skills (e) attributed to him

(4) Find two hidden words in each of the given words.
(a) lifetime (b) outstanding (c) began (d) conqueror (e) father

(D) Activities based on grammar:

(1) Write the correct verb + present / past participles for the following words.
(a) write (b) flourish (c) consider (d) attribute (e) administer (f) play

(2) Use the following words and their homonyms in two separate sentences. *(Note: Homonym is a word that is spelt like another word or pronounced like it but which has different meanings. For example: can means 'be able' and can also mean 'put something in a container'.)*
(a) model (b) veena (c) father

(3) This great Gupta king was not only a great conqueror but also an outstanding diplomat.
(Rewrite the sentence without using 'not only.... but also....')

(4) Samudragupta was the greatest among all the Gupta rulers.
(Rewrite using the comparative form)

(5) The king always worries about the need to educate.
(Replace the infinitive with a gerund) ***(Note: Infinitive is the basic form of a verb such as 'read', 'be' 'run', etc. Gerund is a past participle of a verb form that functions as a noun ending in '– ing'.)***

(6) Use the words 'walking' and 'travelling' to create present participle and gerund sentences.

(E) Answer the following personal response questions:

(1) Think about any other ruler you have learnt from ancient Indian history or any other period. Provide some information about him/her.

(2) According to you, what qualities must a good king possess/exhibit?

(3) What are our duties towards preservation or conservation of any historical site?

(F) Read and understand the above passage well to write a short summary on it. Suggest a suitable title.

NINE
VISUALIZING

Similarly, as a discoverer has to visualize an idea before bringing it to life, we too can visualize the life we hope and want by imagining how we want our mornings to be. After you open your eyes each morning, I want you to analyse yourself as your best self. Imagine you waking up in the morning well rested, healthy, refreshed and full of vigour. Think about the bright blue skies and warm morning sunlight entering through the partly opened window of your room. The birds are pleasantly chirping on a fruit tree just next to your window. As your feet touch the ground, you feel a sense of blessings and gratitude for having yet another day in your life. A person should feel thankful and say, "I am grateful, delighted and excited for today." See yourself brushing your teeth, taking your own sweet time, being patient and careful to brush every tooth. As you go into the shower, visualize yourself feeling calm, composed and easy. After coming out of the shower, because you chose what you were going to wear the night before, it is not a bother to dress. Now see yourself in a determined manner saying to self, "My main aim today is to stay attentive and focused. My goal is to stay away from any danger and have self-control and be orderly."

Visualize your entire morning again as genuinely as possible. You may feel more fresh and fuelled by removing some time for exercise and/or meditation. Believe it, feel it and welcome good practices in your life. Now visualize yourself continuing the day as your best self. Encourage yourself to motivate and uplift others, lead and guide them, share with others, learn from others, patiently listen to them and be progressive and unbiased towards others. More importantly, you must respect their feelings, reactions and views. See yourself in this energetic environment, giving and receiving your best.

Now visualize yourself coming back home at the end of the day. You are surely tired but happy too. You want to sit down and relax. At the same time, you want to be grateful for whatever you have in life: a good satisfying job, a healthy life, loving family, helpful friends and a roof on your head. You possess more than several other dismayed, distressed and destitute people. See yourself in the evening, spending time meaningfully coming up with better ideas and plans for your progress and happiness.

After a long hard working day, when you visualize yourself getting into cozy bed for a good night sleep, see yourself looking up saying, "I am grateful for today. I will wake up tomorrow feeling healthy, energized and refreshed. Thank you Almighty." The truth is that life keeps messing up your plans. How can one guarantee that tomorrow will go the exact way you have already visualized? However, visualizing does not change your life, but it surely changes how you see it. Strong faith provides a viewpoint. It may carry a prayer, an ambition and a resolve that has the potential for a liberating tomorrow from different man-made crises.

English Question Quarters

(A) Solve the following activities:

(1) Consider the list of various things that the writer has narrated in the passage. Rearrange them in the order of their occurrence in the passage. Read the passage again if you are uncertain.

(a) As our feet touch the ground, we feel a sense of blessings and gratitude.

(b) Exercise and/or meditation makes us feel fresh and energetic.
(c) Life keeps messing up our plans.
(d) A person can visualize his/her life as he/she hopes and wants.
(e) Before going for a shower, feel calm, composed and easy.
(f) After reaching home, one wants to sit down and relax.

(2) Fill in the blanks with the correct alternatives:
(a) A ______________ visualizes an idea before bringing it to life. (person / discoverer / visualizer)
(b) The writer guides having a _____________ and orderly intentions. (genuine / meaningful / self-controlled)
(c) We must see ourselves in an energetic ______________. (positivity / environment / condition)
(d) Visualizing does not change life, but it surely changes how we ______________. (see it / choose it / spent it)

(B) Answer the following questions in a few sentences:
(1) Write in your words the manner in which the writer has described morning in the passage.
(2) How does one feel as soon as feet touch the ground? What must a person say in their mind?
(3) Based on the passage, describe in your words the activities from brushing to dressing.
(4) According to the writer, we must encourage ourselves. In what way?
(5) For what we must be grateful for? Why?

(C) Activities based on vocabulary:

(1) Pick out at least five examples of concrete nouns from the passage. *(Note: Concrete nouns are those nouns that can be touched, seen or sensed through our five senses: smell, touch, sight, hearing or taste.)*

(2) Pick out at least five examples of abstract nouns from the passage. *(Note: Abstract nouns are those nouns that cannot be touched or seen. In simpler words, a noun denoting an idea, quality or state rather than a concrete object.)*

(D) Activities based on grammar:

(1) I went to bed. Soon I fell asleep. *(Begin the sentence with 'No sooner... than ...')*

(2) Strong faith provides a viewpoint. *(Rewrite beginning with 'A viewpoint')*

(3) He said, "What kind of visualization do you like?" *(Rewrite using the indirect form of narration)*

(4) She didn't engross into her creative thoughts until recently. *(Rewrite without 'didn't')*

(5) You want to <u>sit down and relax</u>. *(Frame a 'Wh-' question to get the underlined part as answer)*

(E) Answer the following personal response questions:
(1) How do you begin and visualize your day?
(2) Do you agree or disagree with the following statement? *(More importantly, you must respect their feelings, reactions and views.)* Justify your stand/answer.
(3) Staying attentive and focused in life is crucial. Elaborate.

(F) Read and understand the above passage well to write a short summary on it. Suggest a suitable title.

TEN

ONLINE SHOPPING: ADVANTAGES AND DISADVANTAGES

Shopping online has become very popular in recent times. It is a process of purchasing goods and services from merchants selling on the internet. Since the emergence of the World Wide Web, merchants have started to sell their products on the internet. Shoppers can visit web stores from the comfort of their homes and shops through their computers and mobile screens. This has totally altered the experience of shopping. Notionpress, Decathlon, Flipkart, eBay, Snapdeal and Amazon are some of the popular and trusted online shopping websites. Thousands of brand new products are sold and delivered daily through such sites.

Online shopping can be done twenty-four hours a day. Searching an online product comparatively saves time and energy. Cheaper deals and better prices are easily available on online stores. One can search any product effortlessly by using the search feature of the website. However, in the store we have to look for the product until we find it. We have to visit crowded places, making shopping laborious. Many people hate to search for a product and stand in a long queue for paying bills. Books, clothing, household appliances, toys, hardware, software, grocery, electronics, etc. are just some of the hundreds of products consumers can buy from an online store.

Advantages such as discount coupons, return, exchange and refunds can be enjoyed by the customer. Customers can read reviews of any product before buying. The photographs of the product from various angles help to purchase the product confidently. When we visit a store, we most likely have to settle for whatever options and prices the shopkeeper decides. This is not the case with online shopping as we have the freedom to compare prices from different vendors.

Shopping online has its disadvantages too. Sometimes online shoppers may face fraud and security threats. The majority of online shoppers are unaware of attacks from the hacker. Some online stores may be unauthentic, gathering cards and other security details of the customers. Another disadvantage includes that we cannot try things on. If we are buying a clothing item, we don't have the liberty to feel the material, try it on and see how it looks on us. Shoppers have no other option but to believe the description provided for the product. Sometimes, product descriptions are cleverly created to make the product more interesting and attractive. There are many other online issues like slow online connectivity and devices infected by the viruses. We can say that to get benefits from online shopping, one has to be a responsible, intelligent and experienced internet user and an online shopper.

English Question Quarters

(A) Read and understand the passage and answer in a word:

(1) Say whether you agree or disagree the following statements:

(a) Online shopping can be done twenty-four hours a day.
(b) One can hardly search a product on the website.
(c) Shopping online is not so popular in recent times.

(d) Shopping online has certain disadvantages too.
(e) The images of products are incompetently created to encourage the customers to buy.

(2) Complete the following:
(a) Merchants have started to sell their products online since...
(b) Visiting various web stores has totally altered the...
(c) Online shopping has the freedom to...
(d) At times, online shoppers have to face...
(e) To get benefits from online shopping, one has to be a...

(B) Answer the following questions in one or in a few sentences:
(1) Name some of the popular and trusted online shopping websites mentioned in the passage.
(2) Name some of the hundreds of products consumers can buy from an online store.
(3) Mention some of the other online issues highlighted in the passage.
(4) Write on a few advantages of online shopping mentioned in the passage.
(5) Write on a few disadvantages of online shopping mentioned in the passage.

(C) Activities based on vocabulary:

(1) Match the meanings in line (a) with the words in line (b).
(a) (i) a person who sells things (ii) taking a lot of time and effort (iii) shoppers with no option (iv) that you cannot believe or rely on (v) an amount of money that is taken of the usual cost of something (vi) a person who buys and sells goods in large quantities

(b) (i) merchant (ii) unauthentic (iii) discount (iv) laborious (v) vendor

(2) Make meaningful sentences using the following words.
(a) online (b) hacker (c) customer (d) shoppers

(3) Choose the correct noun forms from those given in the brackets.
(a) enjoy (enjoyment / enjoyable)
(b) effortlessly (effortless / effort)
(c) responsible (responsive / responsibility)
(d) intelligent (intelligence / intelligently)

(D) Activities based on grammar:

(1) We were designing the first online shopping website.
(Name the tense of the underlined part to include time and aspect) ***(Note: The Past Continuous (Progressive) Tense is used to denote an action on at some time in the past.)***

(2) The boy shopped online.
(Change it into passive voice) ***(Note: A sentence in which the subject does the action is said to be the Active Voice and a sentence in which the subject is not the doer (one that does) but the receiver of the action is said to be the Passive Voice.)***

(3) Delzin was helping her grandmother.
(Change the voice)

(4) The videography of the product from a few angles help to purchase the product timidly.
(Rewrite the correct sentence by rectifying the error)

(5) Write three sentences of your choice containing Adverb clause of purpose. ***(Note: Adverb clause of purpose is introduced by the subordinating conjunctions like... lest, so that and in order that. In order that and lest are used in a sentence in a formal style.)***

(E) Answer the following personal response questions:

(1) According to you, online or the traditional way of shopping is better, easy and convenient. Why?
(2) At some or the other point of time you must have surely done online shopping. Were you satisfied or dissatisfied with it? Share your experience.
(3) Other than, those mentioned in the passage, name a few online shopping websites you know.

(F) Read and understand the above passage well to write a short summary on it. Suggest a suitable title.

ELEVEN

MOTIVATION: THE MASTER OF SUCCESSFUL LIFE

Being successful is very important for everyone. It is the basic need of a human to gain recognition, dignity, money, power, position and fame. However, in order to be successful, one needs to be highly dedicated, disciplined and motivated. Motivation thrives towards success.

Have you ever been forced to do some work that your heart does not permit? You must have responded to such work neither passionately nor positively. Now compare such work to some other work that you like to perform the most and see the difference in your attitude. Which one was accomplished quickly and with a better outcome? Of course, the task you liked performing the most. This is what motivation is all about. It serves as a start-up so that you can get ahead with the work. The most testing phase of any task is to get it started. Once things get started, there is no turning back. Soon, motivation becomes a key factor in making the person get started towards attaining success.

In search of success, a person may not be always rewarded with success. Life hits you in the head and one has to fall down many times before getting up and moving ahead. After all, obstacles are essential in making a person strong. It makes us worthy of success. So, it is important to be mentally prepared to face the tough work, the challenges and the problems in order to move forward. Keeping yourself motivated all the time in order to keep pushing and going ahead is very important.

What successful people do that some of us do not? People always wonder about this and fail to find the answer. It is the extra hard work they do that makes them successful. Even if you have started up, moved on and faced challenges, you still need to push it beyond what your normal capacities are, only then you can yield the fruits of sweet success. The road to success is hard, long, laborious, boring and tiresome, but if we have motivation as our dependable buddy, then there is no need to worry about anything. Difficult times can be endured through motivation. Being motivated safeguards that you not only do it the right way but also enjoy yourself moving forward. Therefore, always feel motivated, keeping hopes alive. Look towards a happier and prosperous future.

English Question Quarters

(A) Fill in the blanks with the correct alternatives:

(1) ____________ thrives individual towards success. (endurance / motivation / money)

(2) ____________ are essential part in making a person strong. (challenges / rewards / obstacles)

(3) A person may not always be rewarded with ____________. (success / position / fame)

(4) The writer in the passage had asked to keep ____________ alive. (capacities/ hopes / goals)

(B) Answer the following questions in one or in a few sentences:

(1) How can one yield the fruits of sweet success?

(2) What is it that successful people do that some of us do not?

(3) Based on the passage, what is the basic need of a human?

(4) What is needed in order to be successful? Who thrives individual towards success?
(5) How is the road to success described? When there is no need to worry?
(6) Write in your words how is the search for success described in the passage?

(C) Activities based on vocabulary:

(1) Write the verb or adjective forms of the given words. State if your answer is a verb or an adjective.
(a) motivation (b) passionately (c) performing (d) accomplished (e) positively

(2) Write the noun or adverb forms of the given words. State if your answer is a noun or an adverb.
(a) passionately (b) quick (c) positive (d) performing (e) successful

(3) Pick out the antonyms of the following words from the passage.
(a) failure (b) bitter (c) behind (d) uninspired (e) interesting

(D) Activities based on grammar:

(1) In search of success, a person may not be always rewarded with success.
(Rewrite beginning with the words 'A person...')

(2) which one was accomplished quickly and with a better outcome
(Punctuate the sentence correctly)

(3) Failures will not be able to stop her.
(Make the sentence Affirmative without changing its meaning) ***(Note: In English grammar, an affirmative statement is any sentence or declaration that is positive in nature.)***

(4) To be successful, one needs to be highly dedicated, disciplined and motivated.
(Rewrite using 'nothing' and change the sentence accordingly)

(5) Life hits you in the head.
(Rewrite in the Present Perfect Continuous Tense)

(6) Find any two sentences in the Present Perfect Tense from the passage.

(E) Answer the following personal response questions:
(1) Is motivation necessary to succeed? Why? Write in your own words what motivates you the most.
(2) Explain the following line from the passage in your own words.... *Life hits you in the head and one has to fall down many times before getting up and moving ahead.*
(3) What do you learn from the above text?

(F) Read and understand the above passage well to write a short summary on it. Suggest a suitable title.

TWELVE

WORLD HEALTH ORGANIZATION

World Health Organization (WHO) a specialized agency of the UN (United Nations) that is responsible for international public health and improving the health standards of the people around the globe. It encourages medical research. The WHO Constitution establishes the governing structure and philosophies of the agency. It states its main objective as, "*the attainment by all people of the highest possible level of health*". It is headquartered in Geneva, Switzerland. It has 6 semi-autonomous regional offices and 150 field offices from various nations.

The WHO was established on 7th April 1948. Every year, this date is observed as World Health Day. The first meeting of the World Health Assembly, which is the governing body of WHO, took place on 24th July 1948. Its board mandate includes supporting worldwide healthcare, observing public health hazards, organizing responses to health crises and promoting human health and welfare. It also provides technical help to those countries that set international health standards, strategies as well as collects data on global health issues through the World Health Survey. The World Health Report as its prominent publication provides expert assessments of global health topics and health statistics of all the nations. This world organization serves as an opportunity for meetings and discussions on world health issues.

The WHO has played a primary role in several public health achievements, notably the eradication of smallpox and polio as well as the development of an Ebola vaccine. Its existing priorities not only include infectious diseases like tuberculosis, AIDS, Ebola and COVID-19, but also non-infectious diseases like heart disease and cancer. It also focuses on healthy diet, nutrition and food security and substance abuse. As a part of the United Nations Sustainable Development Group, the organization is composed of representatives from 194 member states.

It also elects and advises an executive board made up of 34 health professionals. The agency summons yearly and is accountable for choosing the Director General. It sets goals and priorities approving its budget and activities. The current Director General of WHO is Tedros Adhanom Ghebreyesus. He is an Ethiopian by origin and the former Health and Foreign Minister of Ethiopia. In May 2017, he began his five-year term at the Seventieth World Health Assembly. He was appointed as the Director General on 1st July 2017. However, for funding, WHO depends on the contributions from member states and its private sponsors. Its total approved budget for 2020-2021 is over 7.2 billion dollars, of which the majority comes from voluntary aid.

English Question Quarters

(A) Choose the correct alternatives and complete the following sentences:

(1) WHO encourages ______________________________

(a) to appoint a new Director General

(b) researches in medical

(c) other world organizations

(d) United Nations Sustainable Development Group

(2) WHO comprises representatives from ____________________

(a) several public health sectors
(b) various nations across the globe
(c) a few nations of the world
(d) 194 member states

(3) The governing body of WHO directed its first meeting of the World Health Assembly on ____________

(a) 1st July 2017
(b) 24th July 1948
(c) 17th May 1946
(d) 7th April 1948

(4) The board of WHO mandates ____________________

(a) support to worldwide healthcare
(b) voluntary assistance
(c) financial assistance
(d) global health topics and health statistics

(B) Answer the following questions in one or in a few sentences:

(1) For what mainly is the World Health Organization responsible?
(2) State the main objective of WHO Constitution.
(3) Where is the headquarters of the World Health Organization situated? Write about its regional and field offices.
(4) Every year, what is observed on 7th April?
(5) Name the prominent publication of the World Health Organization. What does it provide?
(6) Describe the public health achievements of the World Health Organization mentioned in the passage. What are its present priorities?
(7) Who is current Director General of WHO? He belongs to which nationality?

(C) Activities based on vocabulary:

(1) Write from the passage words for...

(a) evolution (b) endorsing (c) specialists (d) maintainable

(2) Find out the antonyms from the passage for the following words.

(a) failures (b) introduction (c) irresponsible (d) omit (e) deteriorating (f) minority

(D) Activities based on grammar:

(1) The Director General of WHO spoke against the idea.
(Rewrite using 'did not')

(2) Recollect any two pairs of words that sound the same/pronounce the same but have different spellings and different meanings. Make suitable sentences with all the four words. ***(Note: Words having different spellings and meanings but are pronounced in the same way are called 'Homophones'. For example... accept/except; new/knew. etc.)***

(3) WHO serving as the opportunity for meetings and discussions in world health issues.
(Spot grammatical errors in the sentence and rewrite it)

(4) Although a few organizations carry power, they are not very tactful.
(Rewrite using 'but')

(5) That is the best thing that has happened to me.
(Underline the subordinate clause and state its kind)

(E) Answer the following personal response questions:
(1) Provide some information about any local organization or a social group around your vicinity who functions for the wellbeing of society.
(2) Give some information on the, functions and aims of any one international agency/organization of your choice.

(F) Read and understand the above passage well to write a short summary on it. Suggest a suitable title.

THIRTEEN

FREEDOM OVER TROUBLES

The bear kept continuing, "We can survive without food and water in winter, for we sleep through the season. I have an ample amount of fat under my skin on which I can feed easily all through the winter. I have nothing to protect myself from the cold and chilling winds besides this fur on my body, which is not enough. What I need is a warm and cozy place to sleep in."

"Why don't you come with me?" the farmer offered. "You will stay warm and will have enough to eat throughout the winter. The only thing you have to do in return is look after my beehives in summer." The bear felt tempted and agreed to the mouth-watering offer instantly. He climbed into the farmer's cart and the farmer took him to his home.

The farmer and his wife took very good care of the bear. He was given a special warm place to stay in their barn. The bear thanked his lucky stars. He had a good place to live in and had enough to eat. He had to do nothing in return until the summer arrived. The bear started to watch over the beehives and had a lick of honey now and then in summer. The animal was very pleased with his comfortable life.

The thick iron chain that he wore around his neck kept him away from going out to wander freely. He missed his freedom to roam anywhere. The bear thought about it repeatedly and one fine morning finally he asked the farmer to let him go for a stroll. The farmer agreed and opened the gates of the barn. After many days, the bear got a chance to stretch himself. He stepped out of the gates and said to the farmer, "Thank you and your wife for the food and shelter, but now I wish to leave." Before the farmer could realize anything, the bear ran straight for his freedom in the forest. "Please," the farmer requested, "Please come." After a while, the bear sat down for some rest under a fruit tree and said to himself: "Freedom, even if it means staying cold and hungry in winter is far better than being in captivity, no matter how well fed and protected you may be!"

English Question Quarters

(A) Read the passage carefully and solve the following activities:

(1) Pick out the false sentences and write them correctly:

(a) The farmer was given a special cold place to stay in the barn.
(b) The bear climbed into the farmer's car.
(c) The bear thanked his lucky stars.
(d) When winter came, the bear started to watch over the birds and had a lick of honey now and then.

(2) Who said the following words to whom and when?

(a) Freedom, even if it means staying cold and hungry in winter is far better than being in captivity, no matter how well fed and protected you may be!
(b) Why don't you come with me?
(c) What I need is a warm and cozy place to sleep in.
(d) Thank you and your wife for the food and shelter, but now I wish to leave.

(e) The only thing you have to do in return is look after my beehives in summer.

(B) Complete the following in your own words. Also, answer the given questions:

(1) The bears can survive without food and water in winter because...
(2) The bear watched over the beehives and...
(3) How did the bear feed himself through the winter?
(4) What condition did the farmer keep before taking the bear to his house?
(5) Describe the stay of the bear at the farmer's house.
(6) Why could the bear not wander freely? What did the bear start to miss?

(C) Activities based on vocabulary:

(1) Pick out the similar meaning words for the word 'stroll' from the passage.

(2) Find the words from the passage for the following.

(a) somewhere to stay – _______________
(b) a person who owns or manages a farm – _______________
(c) a sweet sticky yellow substance made by bees – _______________
(d) a farm structure for storing grain or keeping animals in – _______________
(e) a vehicle with two or four wheels pulled by animal/s – _______________

(3) Find the meanings of the following words/phrases and create meaningful sentences of your choice.

(a) mouth-watering (b) his lucky stars (c) instantly (d) cozy (e) wander

(D) Activities based on grammar:

(1) Make two sentences by using the word 'water' as a noun and as a verb, without altering its form.

(2) The bear had to focus on what to eat.
(Rewrite using the Simple Future Tense)

(3) The animal was very happy with his comfortable life.
(Find and underline the adjective)

(4) He had to do nothing in return <u>until the summer arrived</u>.
(Rewrite the sentence beginning with the underline part)

(5) "Please," the farmer requested, "Please come." *(Rewrite in indirect speech)*

(E) Answer the following personal response questions:

(1) Will you like if someone hinders your freedom while providing all the other comforts of life?
(2) The bear has shown his helplessness as well as his happiness. Support your answer by picking up the respective lines from the passage.
(3) Do you agree or disagree in encroaching the freedom of birds by caging them for fun and past time? If not, why?

(F) Read and understand the above passage well to write a short summary on it. Suggest a suitable title.

FOURTEEN

FOSSILS

The fossils are a record of the life that lived very long ago. The record confirms that most of the species existing today are very different from the fossil species. The facts about the animals and plants that existed long ago can be studied from their fossils. Fossils are the remains of animals and plants that become hard over time and turn into rocks. A fossil is an important piece of evidence from pre-historic times. Some of the important examples of fossils are wood replaced by minerals, bones preserved in tar pits, impressions of a leaf or stem in a rock, an insect trapped in firm and stiff plant sap and an animal trapped and frozen in the ice.

Most of the fossils were formed at the bottoms of the shallow seas covered under a large part of the earth. Numerous plants and animals died in the shallow waters. After their death, they were settled at the bottom. Gradually, they were covered by sand and mud. However, the change took hundreds and thousands of years. In a few cases, a plant or animal may have left only an imprint in the rock and in a few other cases; they may have been completely covered. When the organism decayed, its outline was left in the material that turned to rock. However, most of the time, the hard parts of an organism such as a bone and/or tooth were preserved. Sometimes the entire organism turned into a fossil.

Fossils almost occur in sedimentary rocks. Sedimentary rocks are types of rocks that are formed by the accumulation or deposition of mineral or organic particles at the earth's surface. Mud, sand and other fine particles at the bottom of the shallow seas are called 'sediments'. The fossil organisms die shortly before the rock begins to form from the sediments. Fossils discovered at the lower layers of rock are usually of organisms older than fossils discovered in the upper layers of rock. The estimated time of the appearance of organisms can be determined by the position of their fossils in the layer of the rock. Thus, the ages of fossils can be determined according to the ages of the rocks where they were found.

English Question Quarters

(A) Fill in the blanks with the correct alternatives:

(1) Dead plants and ____________ were covered by sand and mud. (animals / fossil / insects)
(2) Numerous plants and animals died in the shallow ____________. (oceans / waters / ice)
(3) The species existing today are very different from the ____________ species. (fossil / rock / organism)
(4) Fossils almost occur in ____________ rocks. (pre-historic / muddy / sedimentary)
(5) Sometimes, the entire ____________ turned into a fossil. (particles / organism / evidence)

(B) Answer the following questions in one or in a few sentences:

(1) What are fossils? What does the record confirm?
(2) Give some of the important examples of fossils.
(3) What are sedimentary rocks?
(4) What are sediments?
(5) What parts of the organisms are preserved most of the time?

(6) How is the estimated time of the appearance of organisms determined?
(7) Where are most of the fossils formed? With what they are gradually covered?

(C) Activities based on vocabulary:

(1) Find the meanings of the following words and create meaningful sentences of your choice.
(a) pre-historic (b) frozen (c) imprint (d) appearance (e) decayed

(2) Pick out from the passage words that mean the following. State if it is a noun or adjective.
(a) the parts of something that are left (b) a group into which animals, plants, etc. are divided (c) something that is present (d) a layer of a substance on rocks or soil (e) existing in large numbers

(3) Pick out any four words from the passage that are formed by using a prefix.

(D) Activities based on grammar:

(1) When the organism decayed, its outline was left in the material that turned to rock.
(Rewrite in your language without changing the meaning)

(2) Until we read about fossils, we hardly think about them.
(Begin the sentence with 'How...!)

(3) He had read a book on fossils.
(Begin the sentence with 'Hadn't...?)

(4) I couldn't possibly understand anything more unless they had some of those incredible pictures of the fossils.
(Rewrite as an affirmative sentence)

(5) (a) We could go on with our excavation if we didn't have to submit our reports tomorrow. (suggestion / condition)
(b) Could I use your book on fossils for my project? (request / possibility)
(c) Instead of playing video games, you could read books to gain knowledge. (ability / suggestion)
(d) Deena could write well in her biography. (past ability / possibility)
(Recognize the different uses of the word 'could' given in the brackets)

(E) Answer the following personal response question:
(1) Fossils become hard over time and turn into rocks. Think about any other long natural process that takes years to form or take place.

(F) Read and understand the above passage well to write a short summary on it. Suggest a suitable title.

FIFTEEN

WISDOM HATCHED IN A PROVERB

It is used as a caution to someone not to plan anything in advance that depends on a certain good thing that is likely to occur in the future. This proverb is used while advising a person in enthusiasm to wait until the good thing actually takes place. It teaches us not to be too sure about something that is expected to happen in future for sure, because it may never happen at all in reality.

Once upon a time, a girl carried a basket of eggs. While she was walking through the forest, she began to think about how many chicks she would have. She also thought about how much money she would make by selling those chicks and the things she would buy with all that money. Her thinking was inevitable. When she was thinking about all this, she slipped and fell down. Her basket of eggs dropped, leaving her with no eggs and chicks. She regretted not being careful while carrying the eggs. Hence, this proverb can be exactly applied to this girl.

Those who purchase lottery tickets, most of them start to think that they are going to win and become wealthy. They begin to hatch plans as to what they are going to do with the prize money. By using this proverb, we can advise them... 'Hold your horses' until the official announcement of the lottery comes out. Thus, when we tell a person not to count the chickens before they are hatched, we are trying to save him from the disappointment and dissatisfaction he may encounter in future. In the same way, when we are told not to make early celebrations of success in business, we are advising the person not to count profits in advance until the money is in the hands. A person must not be too enthusiastic and optimistic about a favourable outcome of his choice. A flower and a bud are the two different things. Until the bud does not blossom into a beautiful flower, we cannot say that the bud will become a flower because it is possible that abruptly it can be plucked by someone. Hence, until it becomes a reality, it is not intelligent to build too much hope on anything that we do. Excessive zeal on something to happen may end in disaster and displeasure.

English Question Quarters

(A) Find two correct statements from the given alternatives for each of the following:

(1) The above passage teaches us to...
(a) purchase a lottery ticket
(b) never be overenthusiastic
(c) carry a basket filled with eggs
(d) not to expect highly favourable result before the actual outcome

(2) The proverb advises a person to...
(a) be not so sure about something that is expected to happen in future
(b) keep very high hopes before it changes into a reality
(c) wait until the good thing actually takes place
(d) calculate profits in advance

(3) A person must not be...
(a) counting his chickens before they are hatched
(b) disaster and displeasure
(c) exactly applied to the girl
(d) too enthusiastic and optimistic

(B) Answer the following questions in one or in a few sentences:
(1) Write in your words what the last sentence in the passage tells us.
(2) What was the girl in the passage thinking?
(3) What advice has the writer given to those who purchase lottery tickets?
(4) In the last paragraph, the writer has used an idiom 'Hold your horses'. What does it mean?
(5) What has the writer said about a flower and a bud?

(C) Activities based on vocabulary:

(1) From the passage, pick out another word for 'zeal'.

(2) Write words ending in '-ity', '-ly' using the words given.
(a) actual (b) real (c) exact (d) inevitable (e) like (f) possible

(3) Find one word each from the passage for the following.
(a) Sadness because something good or successful has not happened.
(b) A well-known phrase or sentence that gives advice.
(c) To break open so that a young bird, fish, insect, etc. can come out of an egg.
(d) A written or spoken statement that informs people about something.
(e) A feeling that you are not pleased and satisfied.

(4) Pick out any three adjectives from the last paragraph of the passage.

(5) Use the words 'beautiful' and 'reality' from the passage in one meaningful sentence.

(D) Activities based on grammar:

(1) Harshada was the smartest girl in the class. *(Change it into comparison degree)*

(2) Harshada was smarter than all the other girls in the class.
(Change it into positive degree)

(3) Recently, I read a very well written proverb in one of the books of Firoz Tata titled 'Augmenting Your Knowledge' and was extremely moved.
(Rewrite as a complex sentence) ***(Note: A complex sentence is made of one main clause and one or more subordinate clauses. Such sentences are easy to recognize as they frequently use subordinating conjunctions such as since, until, because, etc. to connect clauses.)***

(4) The teacher praised the girl for her attentiveness.
(Rewrite as a compound sentence) ***(Note: A compound sentence is made of two or more coordinate clauses that are joined by coordinating conjunction like but, neither...nor, or, either...or, not only...but also, etc.)***

(5) The girl in the purple skirt is my friend.
(Pick out the subject, verb and predicate)

(6) Selling eggs worth two hundred rupees per week doesn't go far.
(Rewrite as an interrogative sentence)

(7) When she was thinking about all this, she slipped and fell down.
(Rewrite beginning with 'While')

(E) Answer the following personal response questions:
(1) According to you, what is a proverb? Do you agree with the proverb 'Do not count your chickens before they are hatched?' What advice does this proverb give?
(2) Write a small paragraph of about fifteen to twenty lines on the proverb 'Birds of a feather flock together'.

(F) Read and understand the above passage well to write a short summary on it. Suggest a suitable title.

SIXTEEN

HEY! IT'S CHRISTMAS TIME

Christmas is a yearly festival honouring the birth of Jesus Christ. It is observed on 25th December as a religious and cultural celebration among billions of people around the world. As Jesus Christ, the founder of the Christian faith was born on 25th December; this day is celebrated as the 'Christmas Day'. It is a holiday to celebrate the birth of Jesus, who, according to the Christian religion, is the son of God. Every year, this day is celebrated with great splendour and joy. Christmas is the same for the Christians as Diwali for the Hindus and Eid for Muslims.

On the day of Christmas, people love to dress themselves in new and colourful clothes. They wish 'Merry Christmas' to their friends, relatives and beloved ones. They visit one another's house to greet and exchange good wishes. Christmas cards, gifts, chocolates, cakes and sweets are sent and received. People are excited for the approaching day and great preparations are done way before. Houses and churches are cleaned and painted. The ceilings and walls are decorated with colourful paper ribbons, flowers, balloons, wall streamers and various decorative articles. The shopkeepers who sell Christmas cards and presents also decorate their shops to attract more customers. Thus, all the Christians whether rich or poor, young or old celebrate Christmas in their own ways.

Usually, the Christmas tree is beautified with small colourful electric bulbs and other tiny pieces of decorative articles like dazzling plastic stars, balls, bells, fairies, mistletoe, etc. Some of the most popular Christmas decorations include candles, garlands, roping, swags, satin ribbons, poinsettias, wreaths, etc. The Christmas tree looks astounding, adding a typical festive mood to the occasion. Delicious cuisines including Christmas pudding and plum cakes are prepared. It is a great day also for the children. They sing the carol in chorus to remember their Lord's birth. They eagerly look for chubby, cheerful, long white-bearded Santa Claus or Father Christmas, often with spectacles, wearing a red coat with white fur collar, white fur-cuffed red trousers, red hat with white fur and black leather belt and boots, carrying a bag full of gifts for children. The Christians all over the world heartily celebrate this festival. In modern times, Christmas is not only much loved and observed by the Christians but also by many non-Christians. They celebrate not as a religious belief, but as an ecstatic occasion.

English Question Quarters

(A) State whether the following statements are true or false:

(1) We celebrate as Christmas on the day when Jesus Christ was born.

(2) God is considered as the son of Christ.

(3) People dress in new and colourful clothes on 25th December.

(4) Delicious cuisines including Christmas pudding and plum cakes are distributed by Santa Claus.

(5) Non-Christians also celebrate Christmas.

(B) Answer the following questions in one or in a few sentences:

(1) Name various Christmas decorations mentioned in the passage.

(2) Usually, how is the Christmas tree decorated?

(3) The writer has beautifully described the appearance of Father Christmas. Write in your own words.

(4) A few delicious Christmas cuisines are mentioned in the passage. Name them.
(5) Name all the religions and festivals stated in the passage.

(C) Activities based on vocabulary:

(1) Spot out the words coming in the passage that are used for Jesus Christ.

(2) A word in the passage, which means 'feeling or displaying great enthusiasm'.

(3) Find antonyms of the following words from the passage.
(a) repel (b) keep (c) miserable (d) daughter (e) subtracting (f) demise

(4) Write from the passage the words or phrases that mean...
(a) so surprising that it is difficult to believe (b) having a good time (c) faith of a religion (d) very famous (e) doing things the way one wants (f) flowers and leaves worn on the head or around the neck

(D) Activities based on grammar:

(1) This day is celebrated with great splendour and joy.
(Rewrite adding a question tag)

(2) It is a great day for the children.
(Rewrite beginning with 'No other...' and make alternate changes)

(3) On Christmas, we <u>love</u> to dress in <u>new</u> and <u>colourful</u> clothes.
(Rewrite using the antonyms of the underlined words)

(4) The family had celebrated Christmas many times.
(Rewrite with Hadn't ...?)

(5) I ordered it to surprise my darling Deena.
(Change the voice)

(E) Answer the following personal response questions:
(1) What preparations do you make for Christmas? How do you spend/enjoy the day? Narrate.
(2) What would you do if you ran short of money to buy a Christmas gift for your sibling?
(3) Would you prefer visiting poor and needy children on the day of Christmas to distribute gifts and sweets among them? Why?

(F) Read and understand the above passage well to write a short summary on it. Suggest a suitable title.

SEVENTEEN

A Fresh Beginning

Once without an invitation wild and malicious wind invaded a peaceful family of innocent little kernels who lived happily and in peace. Before they could understand, the wicked wind abducted one of the defenceless little seeds and carried it away with it until it got weary and fed up with its entire adventure.

The wild wind dragged the little kernel onto a strange and alien seashore. Alone and lost, it kept rolling across a concrete pavement until it was stopped by a dry crevice in the barren cement. Soon an unintended, unknown, unfriendly heel of a leather boot stepped on the little one, jamming it deep in the crack. The kernel was trapped like an imprisoned refuge. It was helplessly separated from its family and now was hopelessly all alone.

One day, deep within the heart of the little fellow stirred a strange, mystical and miraculous life force, which decided to test the death. The dying heart of the confined kernel cried out, "Perhaps, I shall live and not die!" Soon the first gentle drop of morning mist oozed into the crack where the seed was trapped. The poor fellow happily greeted and absorbed the cool pleasant moisture. In a few moments, little wisps of dust moved by the light breeze slipped into the crack to blanket the stranded seed. The seed once again cried, "I shall take root and grow!"

Quietly petite hairy roots were born, finding more moisture and nourishment in the tiny buried cave. The seed got swollen with confidence and determination. Bursting with a new life, it broke wide open. On a bright sunny morning, a little blade of grass popped out of the crack and smiled at the shining sun. It thanked the light rain and waved at the jealous wind. It proudly declared, "Here I come by paving my path against impossible odds! And you too can!"

If this tiny fellow could make it, don't you think that you too can? Every end leads its way towards a new beginning. What may appear like an end may be just the night before the dawning of a fresh dream and a new opportunity. You have within you the power to turn ends into transformations. Just as the helpless seed broke through the concrete to raise its head to the bright new world, so you too can break through to a new and wonderful life.

English Question Quarters

(A) Read the passage carefully and solve the following activities:

(1) The teacher will write a few incomplete sentences on the board and will ask the students to complete them in their own words:

(a) The narrator has described the wind as...

(b) The heel of a leather boot was...

(c) It stirred deep within the heart of the little kernel...

(d) We get a message in the proud declaration of the little fellow that...

(e) A new beginning results from...

(2) Based on the passage, correct the false statements given below:

(a) The seed got tiny yet swollen with water and determination.

(b) There is no power to turn ends into transformations.

(c) The happy heart of the not so confident kernel cried out.
(d) The gentle wind abducted the little seed.

(B) Answer the following questions in one or in a few sentences:
(1) Who lived happily? What happened to them?
(2) What did the wicked wind do? Until when?
(3) Where did the wild wind drag the little kernel?
(4) What oozed into the crack?
(5) Whom did the seed happily greet?
(6) Read the last paragraph of the passage again. What do you learn from it? Write it in your words.

(C) Activities based on vocabulary:
(1) Pick out as many adjectives as possible from the first paragraph of the passage.
(2) Pick out the describing words in the passage used for seed.
(3) Search as many hidden words as possible in the word... 'understand'

(D) Activities based on grammar:

(1) He is interested in learning all about the little seed.
(Pick out the gerund and use it in your own sentence)

(2) Write the present and past participles of the verbs 'drop' and 'break'.

(3) It appears as if the seed will win the battle.
(Frame a 'Wh-' question to get the underlined part as answer)

(4) "Here I come by paving my path against impossible odds!" the seed said.
(Rewrite using the indirect form of narration)

(5) The little seed was really happy.
(Rewrite as an exclamatory sentence)

(E) Answer the following personal response questions:
(1) Mention some of the qualities you noticed in the little seed. Which is your best quality?
(2) Do you find any correlation between our and the life of the little seed? What?

(F) Read and understand the above passage well to write a short summary on it. Suggest a suitable title.

EIGHTEEN

THE BRAIN

The human brain is the central organ of the human nervous system. There are about ten billion nerve cells in the human brain. Brain functions as a major controller of our body. It is made of soft tissues, which includes grey and white matter. This matter contains the nerve cells, small blood vessels and non-neuronal cells that helps to maintain neurons and brain health. The organ has a high water content and almost 60% of fat.

A brain comprises three major parts. They are cerebrum, cerebellum and medulla. The cerebrum is located in the upper part of the head and it is the largest part of the human brain. The intelligence of an individual largely depends on a highly developed cerebrum. The cerebrum is the actual origin of our thinking and alertness. Moreover, it also controls our memory, learning and some voluntary movements of the body. Cerebrum also regulates hearing, seeing, touching, tasting and smelling abilities of an individual. Brain surgeries on humans have revealed the location of control areas with the cerebrum. If any one of these areas are damaged, the sense or activity it regulates is lost.

The cerebellum is a major structure of the hindbrain that is located near the brainstem. It is much smaller and lies behind and below the cerebrum. Its major function is to maintain the balanced senses of the body, meaning this part of the brain is responsible for coordinating voluntary movements. Muscular activities like walking, cycling, running and swimming are also coordinated by the cerebellum. It is also responsible for a number of functions including motor skills such as balance and posture. Muscle coordination by the cerebellum helps a player to make the complex body motions required for a particular sport.

The medulla is the smallest part of the brain. It is located at the base of the skull, just below the cerebellum. The medulla is connected with the spinal cord. It regulates heartbeat, breathing, muscular action of the digestive tract and the secretion of certain glands. These are the unnoticed activities occurring in a human body, unless we decide to think about them. As the breathing and heartbeat rates increase automatically when we are involved in any physical activity, medulla helps in controlling. Moreover, all nerve fibers connecting the brain and spinal cord pass through the medulla. It also regulates certain reflexes like sneezing, coughing, vomiting and swallowing.

English Question Quarters

(A) Read and understand the passage and answer in a word:

(1) Say whether you agree or disagree the following statements:

(a) The human brain is the vital organ of the human nervous system.
(b) The medulla is the biggest part of the brain.
(c) The cerebellum is the actual origin of our thinking and alertness.
(d) Muscular activities are coordinated by the cerebrum.
(e) Brain functions as a major controller of the body.

(2) Name the following:

(a) It determines the intelligence of a person ________________

(b) It comprises three major parts ________________
(c) It controls memory ________________
(d) It regulates one's breathing and heartbeat rates ________________
(e) It is located near the brainstem ________________

(B) Answer the following questions in one or in a few sentences:
(1) In what context the writer in the passage has made the use of the word 'matter'. Explain.
(2) In how many parts is the human brain divided? Name them.
(3) What is the role of cerebrum in the human brain?
(4) Where is the cerebellum located?
(5) What is the role of cerebellum in the human brain?
(6) Where is the medulla located? With what it is connected?
(7) What is controlled by the medulla?

(C) Activities based on vocabulary:

(1) Match the words in line (a) with those in line (b).
(a) (i) hindbrain (ii) sneezing (iii) ten billion (iv) 60% (v) cycling

(b) (i) nerve cells (ii) muscular activity (iii) medulla (iv) human body (v) fat (vi) cerebellum

(2) Find the meanings of the following words and by using them create meaningful sentences of your choice.
(a) brain (b) spinal cord (c) skull (d) brainstem (e) glands (f) coordinate

(3) Write from the passage words that indicate sports.

(4) Pick up at least three the adverbs from the passage.

(5) Make a list of as many words as possible from the passage that are related to the human body.

(D) Activities based on grammar:

(1) The medulla is connected with the spinal cord.
(Pick up the preposition)

(2) Say whether the given sentences are assertive, imperative, interrogative or exclamatory.
(Note: Imperative sentences are used to issue a command, warning, instruction, make a request or offer advice. They tell people what to do. On the other hand, Assertive sentences express strong opinions or desires with self-assurance and confidence without being aggressive so that people take notice.)
(a) We have studied the human brain.
(b) Which activities are coordinated by the cerebellum?
(c) What a great task it is to understand the human brain!
(d) Always be nice to poor and needy people.
(e) What have you studied about the human brain in medical college?
(f) Certainly, science has made progress in understanding the functioning of the brain.
(g) How wholly we have succeeded in learning about the brain!
(h) Let us study together.

(3) He <u>will</u> somehow <u>understand</u>.

(Rewrite changing to the Past Perfect Tense of the underlined words)

(4) Pick out the finite *(limited by the number or person of the subject)* or non-finite Verbs *(not controlled by the subject, number or person)* from the following sentences.

(a) He decides to visit a doctor.

(b) The child continued to study.

(c) I request you to answer my questions.

(d) I have come to you to ask you to answer a couple of questions on the human brain.

(5) There are thousands of intelligent brains all over the country.

(Pick out the determiners and write them) ***(Note: A Determiner is a word that appears before a noun or a noun phrase to show how the noun is being used.)***

(E) Answer the following personal response questions:

(1) Have you ever read any book on the science of the human body? Name it. State couple of the most interesting facts that you came across in the book.

(2) What qualities/skills do you think are needed to become a good brain surgeon?

(F) Read and understand the above passage well to write a short summary on it. Suggest a suitable title.

NINETEEN
The Animal Kingdom

There are more than 1.5 million different kinds, shapes, sizes and colours of animals on our planet. They survive in different kinds of places and behave in very different ways. However, the enormous Antarctic blue whale is the biggest animal on the planet, weighing up to 400000 pounds, meaning approximately 33 elephants. It reaches up to 98 feet in length. Some animals are as small as tiny spots of dust. The Kitti's hog-nosed bat is regarded as the world's smallest mammal at 1.1 inches.

Animals may appear very different, but they are alike in several ways. They all breathe, feed and grow in their own ways. Most of the animals have senses so that they can see, hear, smell, taste and touch what is around them. They use their senses to hunt as well as defend. For instance, owls have large eyes that are used to prey at night. Many animals breathe using lungs.

Animals cannot make their own food like plants. They have to find something to eat in their surroundings. They move to find food, to save themselves from being killed or to find a partner. Animals have various ways of having babies. Some give birth to their young ones, while others, such as birds and reptiles like crocodiles and tortoises lay eggs from which the young ones hatch.

Animals can be classified into two categories of vertebrate and invertebrate. Vertebrate animals have backbones that run down the backs of their body. The invertebrates do not have backbones. Birds, reptiles, amphibians, fish and mammals are all vertebrates. Their bones make up their skeleton. The skeleton supports the animal's body and the muscles that are used to move around. A snail is an invertebrate. It has a shell that protects its soft body. Jellyfish are invertebrates that live in water. They can even survive out of water by collapsing into a wobbly lump of jelly. Jellyfish are the oldest multi-organ animal.

The things that animals do is part of their behaviour. Certain behaviours have to be learnt by observing and monitoring them. Many animals like wolves and lions use sound to communicate. By their unique sounds, they tell their rivals to stay away. Wolves howl to communicate while lions roar.

The place where an animal lives is called its habitat. A habitat is made up of a group of plants and animals. Mountains, seas and forests are some of the many different types of natural habitats. The sea is considered as the world's biggest habitat. As forests are full of trees, they offer animals a lot of space to make a home and plenty of food to eat. Even a pile of logs is home to many different animals like centipedes, slugs and woodlice.

A food chain is a series of living creatures in which each type of creature feeds on the one below it in the series. Insects are fairly lower down the food chain. All animals rely on other living things for food. Some animals eat plants and grass, while others hunt the plant-eater animals. Each food chain begins with plants.

Animals that only eat plants are called herbivorous. Because of their plant diet, herbivorous animals typically have mouthparts adapted to crushing or grinding. Cows, goats, tortoises, horses, gorillas, deer, elephants, etc. are some of the herbivorous animals. On the other hand, wolves, lions, leopards, hyenas, polar bears, cheetahs, etc. are carnivorous animals as they hunt other grazing animals. Thus, a carnivore is an organism that mostly eats meat or the flesh of animals. Sometimes carnivores are called 'predators'.

English Question Quarters

(A) Based on the passage, the teacher will write a few incomplete sentences on the board and will ask the students to complete them:

(1) The Antarctic blue whale is the...
(2) The weight of the planet's biggest animal is compared to...
(3) Large eyes helps...
(4) Vertebrate and invertebrate are the...
(5) Observation and monitoring is necessary to...

(B) Answer the following questions in a few sentences:

(1) Among animals, what are the various ways of having babies?
(2) How are animals classified?
(3) Name the world's smallest mammal. How much does it measure?
(4) Which animals are considered as vertebrates? Give examples.
(5) Which animals are considered invertebrates? Give examples.
(6) Of what a habitat is made up? Give examples.
(7) What is a food chain? Explain.
(8) Explain the terms 'herbivorous' and 'carnivorous' with examples.

(C) Activities based on vocabulary:

(1) Pick out any ten names of the animals mentioned in the passage.

(2) The following compound words from the passage are spelt in jumbled order. Rearrange the letters to make them meaningful.

(a) i c t a c r n t a ________________ (b) p e l e a h t n ________________ (c) v o r i b r e h u o s ________________
(d) e t a r b e t r e v n i ________________ (e) p h b i m a i n a ________________

(3) Classify the given words... (different, colour, enormous, example, habitat, natural, behaviour, wobbly, soft, animal) into adjectives and nouns. Use the given words to create meaningful sentences of your own.

(4) Name the sounds of two carnivorous animals mentioned in the passage.

(D) Activities based on grammar:

(1) Some animals are as small as tiny specks of dust.
(Pick out the determiner)

(2) Some animals are as small as tiny spots of dust.
(Rewrite using 'a few' and 'like')

(3) They can even survive out of water.
(Make the sentence affirmative)

(4) Have you ever seen an Antarctic blue whale?
(Make the sentence assertive)

(5) Choose the correct 'not only.... but also'.... from the given sentences.

(a) Not only do they move to find food to save themselves from being killed but also.
(b) They move to find food not only but also to save themselves from being killed.
(c) They not only move to find food but also to save themselves from being killed.
(d) But also, they move to find food not only to save themselves from being killed.

(E) Answer the following personal response questions:

(1) Imagine a visit to the forest. With what you encountered? Describe it in at least fifteen to twenty lines.
(2) Write about any one of your favourite domestic animals.

(F) Read and understand the above passage well to write a short summary on it. Suggest a suitable title.

TWENTY
THE KINDNESS ALWAYS RETURNS

Later that evening, once again he cut out the leather for four pairs and left it on his wrecking table. The next morning, he went to his belongings to start the work. He was again stunned to see four pairs of new, beautiful shining boots all ready to sell. This went on for many days. Soon the bootmaker became rich. His boots were so well made that the King, his Queen and several royal people loved to buy them.

Now time came to find out who was making the boots for him. "We must find out the real bootmaker," said the father to his daughter. Thus, one bright moonlit night both decided to hide themselves in the house, to keep an eye on the table. Just when the clock struck 12, three fat dwarfs in torn worn-out clothes and bare feet jumped in through the broken window. They went hopping, singing and dancing up to the bootmaker's table. They sat down and began their magical work with the leather. Their needles flew fast back and forth, back and forth. Their little mallets beat *thapak-thak, thapak-thak*! Before the bootmaker and his daughter could think anything, boots were already made. Soon, the three fat dwarfs hopped out of the broken window.

The next morning the bootmaker said to his daughter, "We should do something for those three dear dwarfs." The daughter knew to stitch clothes. "I would love to stitch some clothes for the kind men as a token of our appreciation." The father agreed at once. He also decided to make a few pairs of boots for the tiny helpers.

Colourful clothes and shiny tiny boots were ready for the gentle souls. They were put on the table with a note, "Thank you dear little angels." So that night father and daughter again decided to hide themselves. Just when the clock struck 12, three fat dwarfs jumped in. They were more than happy to see small clothes and tiny shiny boots for them. They happily slipped into their gifts. They understood that their job was done and so they jumped out of the window and vanished in the dark. After this, the bootmaker and his daughter never saw the little chaps again, and until today good fortune seemed always to be on their side.

English Question Quarters

(A) Read the passage carefully and solve the following activities:

(1) Pick out the false sentences and write them correctly:

(a) The daughter knew to stitch clothes.
(b) Their little mallets beat *thapak-thak, thapak-thak*!
(c) The two fat dwarfs in nice new clothes with tiny boots jumped in through the broken window.
(d) The clothes were so badly made that the King, his Queen and a few royal people hated to buy them.

(2) Who said the following words to whom?

(a) We must find out the real bootmaker.
(b) I would love to stitch some clothes for the little men as a token of our appreciation.
(c) We should do something for those three dear dwarfs.

(3) After reading the passage, put the following events in correct order.

(a) The dwarfs jumped out of the window and vanished in the dark.
(b) The father decided to make a few pairs of boots for the tiny helpers.
(c) "Thank you dear little angels".
(d) The next morning, he went to his belongings to start the work.
(e) The little mallets beat *thapak-thak, thapak-thak*!
(f) Good fortune seemed always to be on the side of the father and daughter.
(g) Three fat dwarfs jumped in through the broken window.
(h) One bright moonlit night both decided to hide themselves in the house.

(B) Answer the following questions in one or in a few sentences:

(1) What went on for many days?
(2) What happened when the clock struck 12?
(3) Describe the magical work of the three dwarfs with the leather.
(4) What did the father and his daughter decide the next morning?
(5) Explain the line, '*They happily slipped into their gifts*'.

(C) Activities based on vocabulary:

(1) Pick up as many words as possible from the passage related to the three dwarfs.
(2) Pick up as many adjectives as possible from the passage that describes dwarfs.
(3) Pick up the words from the passage describing the happy actions of the dwarfs.
(4) Find a word from the passage that means 'to disappear'.

(D) Activities based on grammar:

(1) The dwarfs understood that their job was done and so they jumped out of the window.
(Rewrite without using 'but' and 'so' as the coordinating conjunctions)

(2) They spent a happy time stitching clothes and making boots.
(Frame 'Wh-' question to get the underlined part as the answer)

(3) "We should do something for those three dear dwarfs", said the daughter.
(Rewrite in indirect speech)

(4) his boots were so well made that the king, his queen and several royal people loved to buy them
(Punctuate as well as correct the sentence accordingly)

(E) Answer the following personal response questions:

(1) If you were in place of the father and his daughter, what would you have done for the dwarfs if they had helped you?

(F) Read and understand the above passage well to write a short summary on it. Suggest a suitable title.

TWENTY-ONE

ANSWER SECTION

1. Time and Priorities

(A) (1) False (2) True (3) False (4) True

(B) (1) diary to plan day-to-day activities.
(2) to assess our abilities, needs and necessities in the long term.
(3) time management.
(4) our stress while improving health.

(C) (1) troublesome, something, outcome, doorway, day-to-day
(2) (a) mismanagement (b) inability (c) immaturely (d) unprofessional

(D) (1) Only a few people do not prefer to keep a diary to plan their day-to-day activities.
(2) Aren't several online planners, digital applications and software available?
(3) When we start to prioritize things in life, the ultimate doorway to success opens.
(4) The techniques of time management are not fixed or rigid.

(E) (1) Yes, I certainly agree with the statement "Time once lost, is lost forever." A person who wastes his/her time in excuses, laziness and idleness can never achieve in life. On the other hand, a person who prioritizes things and efficiently manages and uses time can flourish and accomplish his desires and dreams.

(2) Yes, I do think that prioritizing things in life can be very helpful. By prioritizing, a person learns to keep his/her problems, tasks, etc. in the correct order of importance, so that he/she can deal with and pay attention to the most essential things. A person can cultivate the habit of preparing a list of all those tasks that are to be done and prioritize.

(3) If a person is not lazy enough to write down his most important everyday doings then maintaining a conventional diary is a very good option. This even helps in not missing the smallest of the smallest tasks that are to be done for the day. In my opinion, such a method helps in holding one back from excessive screen time and analyses his/her priorities with a calm head.

(4) Such is the statement made when one discovers that he/she is suffering from a fatal illness. Being in eye to eye with death, a person realizes how little time is left on earth in order to display the true potential. Many of us spent most of our lives following the instructions and decisions of others. We should spend every moment of our life trying to discover our own perspective and regulate our own resolve and path in life.

(F) Your time and your priorities

The methods of positively or negatively managing time completely depends on the person. For fruitful and superlative results, one has to look for the practices that best suit them. The main key towards our success is how wisely and effectively we use our time. Grumbling to have a lack of time to do various things is not what a successful individual will ever say. With commitment, patience and self-control, he/she creates the best of his/her content, happy and prosperous personal as well as professional life. Staying focused and having a clear mind is vital. This helps in determining the direction towards important goals in life. Moreover, clear priorities will visualize what is more important to us, and things that require our instant attention. Prioritizing would also help us to assess our capabilities, desires and requirements in the long term. Maintaining a diary is a better option to think and write down a list of things that require our attention. Therefore, efficient time management and prioritizing is surely a more satisfying way to lead a peaceful and prosperous life.

2. Sumo

(A) (1) *dohyo* (2) amateur wrestlers (3) a pyramid

(B) (1) the national sport of Japan.

(2) determine who has stepped out or touched down first.

(3) The main object of the sumo sport is to force the opponent wrestler out of the *dohyo*, which is the center circle of the elevated cement-hard clay ring. In other words, force the opponent to touch the surface of the *dohyo* with any part of his body other than the soles of his feet.

(4) The Japan Sumo Association has officially listed 82 winning techniques consisting of assorted lifts, shoves, throws, trips and pulls. Almost 48 of them are considered as the 'classic' techniques.

(5) Distinctive to sumo is the use of a bellyband or belt called a *mawashi*. A firm two-handed grip on the opponent's *mawashi* is generally practiced in the sport while blocking him from getting a similar grip on his.

(C) (1) (a) opponent (b) amateur (c) determine
(2) (a) sumo wrestling (b) referees dressed like them

(D) (1) (a) She has an angelic face. (noun) (b) We will face (verb) all the challenges together.
(2) (a) According to me, no other wrestler is as great as Hakuhō Shō.
(b) Hakuhō Shō is more talented than most other wrestlers are.
(c) Hakuhō Shō is the most brilliant one in the sumo tournament.
(3) (a) excited (b) great (c) slowly
(4) We have a dozen experienced coaches as well as several strong sumo wrestlers to participate in the competition.

(E) (1) Last month on one of the sports channels I saw a sumo-wrestling match fought between two gigantic wrestlers. One was from Japan and the other was from the UK. They were extremely huge in size, super heavy and very powerful. With their unique techniques and enormous strength, they tried to force one another to touch the surface of the *dohyo* with any part of the body other than the soles of their feet. They had a firm two-handed grip on each other's *mawashi* while blocking the other from getting a similar grip. It was a thrill to watch such a fantastic match.

(2) As a young boy/girl I am very fond of sports and games. The game I like the most is cricket. This game was first introduced by the Englishmen and later it spread to other countries such as Australia, New Zealand, India, Sri Lanka, Pakistan, West Indies, etc. Now more and more countries are beginning to enjoy this wonderful game. Test matches, One Day International matches and modern day T-20 matches are the three forms of cricket matches that are played. There are eleven players in each team and the umpiring in the match is done by three umpires. The captain who wins the toss decides whether his team will have batting or bowling. The team that makes the maximum number of runs is declared as the winner. I enjoy both playing as well as watching cricket. Every evening I go to the school playground for training. Our coach believes that I can become a good fast bowler. I work very hard on my game and hope to represent my country one day. That will be the proudest moment of my life.

(3) The legendary Ghulam Mohammed is my most favourite wrestler of all time. In 1902, Sultaniwala was challenged by a 19-year old wrestler. Although Sultaniwala showed aggression from the start, the teenager blocked all his attempts. Finally, the match was stopped after an hour and the contest ended in a draw. This encounter resulted in the emergence of Ghulam Mohammad, also called 'Gama'. After the epic fight, prominent wrestlers of the sub-continent challenged Gama, but none could succeed. In 1910, Gama and some other wrestlers set sail for England with an eye on winning the World Championship. A match was arranged between him and an American wrestler Doc Roller. In no time, Gama succeeded in defeating him. His next fight was against a leading wrestler from Poland named Stanislaus Zbyszko. He was known to possess a vast knowledge of holds that could impose great pain over the opponent. In 1910, both fought the World Championship battle in London. Stanislaus found that Gama was too fast and shrewd to be caught. Fearing defeat, Stanislaus adopted the strategy of falling to the floor and hugging the mat. This prevented Gama from applying his dangerous strongholds on him. As Stanislaus failed to show up for a rematch in the coming week, the match was awarded to Gama. The great Gama also defeated many of the best wrestlers of the world at that time including European champion Johann Lemm and French champion Maurice Deriaz. In 1933, he returned to India representing that he was one of the greatest wrestlers of the world. He is the only wrestler not to have been defeated even once in his entire career.

(F) The sumo sport (or) The *Yokozuna* sport

Japan is famous for various sports and sports-related events. Sumo wrestling is one of them. Many people consider sumo as the national sport of Japan. The sport has its fame as a spectator sport and each month tournaments are organized. The wrestler's main objective is to force his opponent out of the *dohyo*. The opponent is forced to touch the surface of the *dohyo* with any part of his body besides the soles of his feet. To decide who has stepped out or touched down first is often extremely tricky. Thus, it requires the closest attention of a referee. The judges sit around the *dohyo* at floor level. 82 winning techniques are officially listed by the Japan Sumo Association and some of them are assorted lifts, shoves, throws, trips and pulls. Almost 48 techniques are regarded as the 'classic' techniques. There is the use of a bellyband or belt called a *mawashi*. A firm grip with both hands on the opponent's *mawashi* is crucial while blocking him from getting a similar grip on his. The grand champions in the sport are called '*yokozuna*'.

3. Flora Saves Herself

(A) (1) Sentences (a) and (d) are false sentences. The correct sentences are... (a) The four friends went to fetch some water from the nearby brook. (d) Flora opposed and kept crying, but her tears had no effect on the scoundrel.

(2) (a) The third friend said these words to the other two friends and Flora.
(b) The rogue disguised as uncle (jeweller from the town) said these words to Flora.
(c) The old woman (rogue's mother) said these words to Flora.
(d) The first friend said these words to the other two friends and Flora.

(e) The second friend said these words to the other two friends and Flora.
(f) The rogue said these words to Flora.
(g) Flora said these words to her three friends.

(B) (1) Flora and her friends went to fetch some fresh water from the nearby brook.

(2) Flora replied to her friends that though she was an orphan girl, she had a rich aunt who lived in the town. She further said that one day when she gets married, her aunt would bring her (Flora) expensive clothes, sweets, money and jewellery placed on a golden platter.

(3) Disguised as a jeweller, the rogue carried with him rich clothes, sweets, money and jewellery on a golden platter.

(4) The old woman (mother of the rogue) was astounded to see the beautiful long hair of Flora. She asked the girl to reveal the secret of her beautiful hair. As Flora was an intelligent and smart young girl, she tactfully replied to the old woman saying that she places her head in a mortar and then caresses it with a pestle, helping her to maintain such an attractive and lengthy hair.

(5) The old woman in the passage is described as silly.

(C) (1) beautiful, young, orphan, gorgeous, poor, smart
(2) rogue, stranger, uncle, cad, cunning, scoundrel, crook, jeweller

(D) (1) Although she had never seen him before but she left with him.
(2) What will she bring?
(3) Though the rogue was attracted to Flora, he could not marry her.
(4) The old woman asked/questioned her (Flora) how she manages such long hair.
(5) Flora opened it to see a stranger standing in front of her. "I am your uncle from the town."

(E) (1) If someone forces me for a marriage against my wish, I will never agree. Relationships are nurtured with love, care, respect and affection and not through fights and force. I would immediately inform my parents and/or elders to help me in such a situation. Perhaps, I will also ask the police to help me out and arrest the individual who troubles me for a marriage against my wish.

(2) If I was in the place of Flora, I would have replied that for now I am not interested in getting married until I complete my education and start earning.

(3) The rogue would return in a few hours and presume that Flora was sitting on the chair dressed as a bride. He would call her name many times but would not get any reply. In anger he would pick up the mortar and hit hard on her head. The old woman would fall bleeding-dead. Soon the rogue would discover that she was his mother. Then furiously he would rush towards Flora's house, but may not find her. After a few days he would again decide to go to the girl's house, but this time with his few rogue friends. Flora would pretend to sleep when they would quietly enter her house. As soon as the cad's friends approached her, she would stab a couple of times with a small knife in their shoulders. Seeing this the rogue would get terrified and would run out of the hut for his dear life to never return again.

(F) Flora: The witty girl

Once upon a time, there lived a beautiful orphan girl named Flora. One day along with her three friends, she went to fetch some fresh water from the neighbouring brook. The four girls were having a casual conversation regarding their marriages. Flora said that she had a rich aunt living in the town, who would bring her clothes, sweets, money and jewellery on a golden platter at the time of her marriage. Unfortunately, a passing rogue heard their conversation. Next day, disguised as a jeweller he went to Flora's hut. Placing on a golden platter, he carried with him the things Flora had narrated. He lied to the girl that he was her uncle. He tricked and asked her to come with him. Unknown from the danger, Flora quickly gathered her things and left with him. The sly man took the girl to his worn-out house in the woods. He revealed the truth that he was not her uncle and wanted to marry her. Soon he left her with his old mother and went out to make arrangements for marriage. The old woman was amazed to see the beautiful long hair of Flora. She asked the girl to reveal the secret of her beautiful hair. Flora thoughtfully answered the old woman that she places her head in a mortar and then caresses it with a pestle, helping her to maintain attractive and lengthy hair. The mindless old woman kept her head into the mortar and asked Flora to strike it with a pestle. Flora immediately hit the pestle on her head. The old woman fainted and Flora fled from the villain's house to save herself.

4. Education

(A) (1) decision-making (2) successful (3) education (4) wealth

(B) (1) One can claim a successful life by his/her wealth, fame, career, assets and most of all through personality.

(2) Education gives us the sense of direction, knowledge, skills and focus. This is needed in order to be successful. Our decision-making abilities heavily depend on our education and level of experience. Education makes us stand out among the others and gives us an edge, self-respect and elegance. Moreover, the chances of having a better-paid jobs and a better career heavily depend on the education we attain.

(3) A good education is regarded as the key to success because it transforms our knowledge, values and outlook towards the path to success.

(C) (1) i – iv, ii – vi, iii – ii, iv – v, v – i
(2) (a) self-respect – No person will give you more love, compassion and <u>self-respect</u> than you can give yourself.
(b) focus – <u>Focus</u> the camera on the child.
(c) career – I am sure, that he will be having a very long and successful writing <u>career</u>.
(d) business – She works in the parlour <u>business</u>.
(e) perceive – The main task of a teacher is to get the students <u>perceive</u> for themselves the association between success and struggles in life.

(D) (1) (a) Wealth, fame, career, assets and personality claims success, don't they?
(b) A good education is the key to success, isn't it?
(c) We cannot just sit down and keep dreaming, can we?
(d) Being born with assets will not make us a successful person, will it?

(2) (a) Education not only gives us the sense of direction and knowledge but also skills and focus to succeed.
(b) Education not only makes us stand out among the others but also gives us an edge, self-respect and elegance.

(3) Therefore, let's <u>walk</u> together in the direction of a good education.
Education is the key <u>to success</u> as it transforms our knowledge.

(4) Let education be created for all.

(E) (1) Children in urban as well as rural areas face many problems that keep them away or diverted from receiving appropriate education. Several children in urban areas face problems such as social networking addiction, pressure of having severe competition, excessive indulgence in playing video games, etc. On the other hand, children in rural areas face extreme poverty, child labour, unhealthy settings, exploitation of various kinds, lack of opportunities and facilities.

(2) (i) I will convince parents of such children to send them to school, showing the benefits of education in life. (ii) I will contact certain Non-Governmental Organizations working in the field of education, asking for their assistance. (iii) If parents agree to send their children to school, I will request my parents and ask them to help such unfortunate children by giving some books, clothes and necessary school stationary.

(3) According to me, of course education is extremely important for a good life. It plays a crucial role in determining the way of life one lives. Most of the time, education helps in making clearheaded correct decisions at the correct time. It makes a person broadminded and sometimes a major contributor in the society. More the people in a country are educated, more the country will be progressive and advance.

(F) Education: A key to success

The success of a person highly depends on the level and equality of education he/she attains. Person's prosperity, reputation, profession, possessions and personality highly rest on his/her education. Some of us presume that people born with wealth are already successful. The truth is, being born with possessions and resources will not make us a successful person until we prove ourselves to be worthy of it. Today, more and more people emphasize on being educated in order to succeed. This is because education gives us the sense of path, information, skills and focus which is essential in order to be successful. Individual's management skills profoundly depend on the level of education and the gaining of the gradual experience. Educated person can be offered with a better remunerated job. However, a long tail of educational degrees would not only land us in a better paying job, but also make us worthy of it to climb each ladder of success. We all should join together and receive as well as spread education as much as possible.

5. Plastic and Environment

(A) (1) tons of plastic bags are manufactured each year.
(2) stop using plastic bags.
(3) killing of wildlife, aquatic and terrestrial animals, hazardous impact on humanity and environment because of its non-biodegradable nature.
(4) they are harmful and deadly for the environment, humans as well as animals.

(B) (1) Winds play an important role in carrying plastic bags to lands, rivers, lakes, beaches, seas, oceans and forests; polluting them in different parts of the world.

(2) Plastic is mistaken by the wildlife as food and gradual choking leads to their slow and painful death. According to certain research, every year nearly a lakh of marine mammals die due to this.

(3) Petroleum is a mineral oil that is found under the ground or the sea. It is used to produce petrol, paraffin, diesel, oil, gas, etc. Petroleum as a major source of energy also helps in generating electricity, heat and light.

(4) Burning plastic is a global problem as it emits toxic gases that are harmful for the atmosphere. It also increases the level of Volatile Organic Compounds in the air. These compounds are organic chemicals that have a high vapour

pressure at ordinary room temperature. Burning plastic causes air pollution as it releases toxic fumes into the air as well as soil.

(C) (1) planet
(2) wind, river, lakes, sea, oceans, forests, wildlife, animals, aquatic, terrestrial, mammals, seabirds, petroleum, mineral oil, petrol, paraffin, diesel, oil, gas, air, land, soil, shorelines, beaches
(3) whale, penguin, sea horse, octopus, jellyfish
(4) wolf, hippo, elephant, lion, dog
(5) (a) wildlife (b) packaging (c) heat (d) breakdown

(D) (1) Plastic bags are one of the most dangerous things we use on our planet.
(2) Every year about one million mammals and seabirds die.
(3) How evident it is!
(4) Present Perfect Continuous Tense
(5) Environmentalists had been advising us.

(E) (1) Yes, I can absolutely stop the use of plastic bags in my everyday life. This I can do by using carry bags made out of paper or cloth. I would encourage as many people as possible around me to avoid the use of plastic bags and make them aware about the hazardous consequences of its usage on planet earth and wildlife. Some of the other actions that I can take to limit the impact of plastic bags on the environment may include taking part in neighbourhood clean-up programs, voluntarily recycling household waste, avoiding littering and unlawful dumping of plastic shopping bags as well as using eco-friendly materials.

(2) I would feel extremely shattered, sad and disheartened if I personally came across an animal suffering due to the consumption of a plastic bag. Without wasting any time, I will try to arrange immediate medical attention for the animal or ask some elder to accompany me to the nearby veterinarian clinic/hospital. I will do everything in my control to save its life.

(3) The public should be educated not to use plastic bags, but to use eco-friendly alternative bags that are made from natural fibres, fabric and paper. This will help in reducing the hazardous problems associated with plastic bag wastes. Moreover, regulation against the indiscriminate use and recycling of waste from plastic bags is strongly recommended. The free sale of plastic bags by retailers should be controlled.

(F) The hazards of plastic bags

More awareness is required to take care of our planet Earth. Plastic bags are one of the most hazardous things used by humans as it causes serious environmental harm. Their use not only creates mess in our surroundings but also pollutes the world. As plastic bags kill aquatic and terrestrial animals, many species are already in danger of extinction. They gulp plastic bags as food, resulting in their slow fatal choking. Research indicates that every year nearly a lakh of marine mammals die due to this. A substance called polyethylene is a kind of petroleum used to manufacture plastic bags. Polyethylene is bad for our environment and potentially toxic for human survival. Petroleum as a major source of energy is used to produce petrol, paraffin, diesel, oil, gas, etc. It also helps in producing electricity, heat and light. Each year as tons of plastic bags are manufactured, tons of petroleum are misused in manufacturing them. Burning plastic produces poisonous gases that harm our atmosphere. Plastic bags take more than a thousand years to breakdown and when they are burned, they release toxic fumes into the air and soil.

6. Cholesterol

(A) (1) the blood, fat and most of the tissues
(2) the supply of oxygen to important parts of our body decreases
(3) the foods of animal origin
(4) regular physical mobility and exercise are essential

(B) (1) a high percentage of cholesterol is present in them

(2) they lead to a healthy life, reducing the health risks

(3) of the blockage of blood flow due to excessive fat and cholesterol deposited on the walls of the arteries

(4) Some of the important warning signs of high cholesterol include shortness of breath, numbness, nausea, slurred speech, chest pain or angina, extreme fatigue or extreme coldness and high blood pressure.

(5) We must avoid foods containing more cholesterol. Fresh green leafy vegetables, fruits, cornflakes, pulses and cereals must be the major part of our daily diet.

(6) The body makes all the cholesterol it needs because the body requires a certain amount of cholesterol to make hormones, vitamin D and substances that help in the digestion of various foods.

(C) (1) (a) hazardous (b) blockage (c) discovered (d) immediately (e) essential
(2) meat, eggs, butter, ghee, cheese, fresh leafy vegetables, fruits, cornflakes, pulses and cereals
(3) noun: body, animal, meat, part, functioning, eggs, consumption
verb: found, decreases, obstructed, prove, include
adjective: healthy, small, only, high, fresh, hazardous
adverb: essentially, especially, regularly, immediately

(D) (1) (a) a (b) an (c) the (d) the (e) a
(2) when the patient arrived – Subordinate clause. Adverb clause of time
(3) Though the doctor listened to the patient, he said nothing.
(4) <u>Fainting</u>, she fell to the ground.
(5) The blood flowed continuously.

(E) (1) If my doctor warns me to keep a check on my wrong lifestyle and eating habits resulting in higher levels of cholesterol in my body, I will immediately follow his advice for a better and healthy living. I will involve myself in some lighter exercises in the beginning such as daily walking for a few minutes, or probably yoga, cycling or swimming. More importantly, I will keep a close watch and control on the food I eat every day. I will try to consume foods that have fibre in them, helping me to reduce my weight. Perhaps, by consulting a professional (nutritionist) I will try my very best to control my increased cholesterol.

(2) It depends on the lifestyle and approach from person to person making it easy or difficult in maintaining his/her good health. However, it is easy for those who understand the concept of health is wealth. According to me, in the times of the internet at our fingertips one can easily assess and gather information on the ways and ideas of maintaining good health by following some of the basic healthy principles in day-to-day life.

(3) To those who are careless with regard to their health... I wish to give them a message that life hardly gives us a

second chance. One must never take their good health for granted. Pleasurable cravings and temptations of various foods gradually ruin our body. Eat simple and healthy in the correct quantity and at the correct time. Help yourself with sufficient exercise and love your body.

(F) Control diet, control cholesterol

Cholesterol was first discovered in 1812. It is a fatty substance found in the blood, fat and most of the tissues in the human body. Cholesterol is vital for normal functioning of the digestive system. However, an increase of cholesterol in the body can be dangerous. The free flow of the blood is blocked when unnecessary fat and cholesterol are deposited on the walls of the arteries. This can prove fatal. Shortness of breath, numbness, nausea, slurred speech, chest pain or angina, extreme fatigue, extreme coldness and high blood pressure are some of the significant warning signs of high cholesterol in the body. A person can regulate his/her cholesterol through the correct diet and medical guidance. As a high percentage of cholesterol is present in the foods from animal sources like meat, eggs, butter, ghee, cheese, etc.; fresh green leafy vegetables, fruits, cornflakes, pulses and cereals must be the major part of one's diet. However, as the body produces the cholesterol it needs, a certain amount of cholesterol is required to make hormones, vitamin D and substances that help in the digestion of different foods. Numerous methods can be followed to maintain the desirable levels of cholesterol in our body. Therefore, for healthy living one must do regular exercise, yoga, cycling, walking and control the intake of fatty foods.

7. In Search of a Hope

(A) (1) (a) A person should believe in himself.
(b) Neither he nor anyone else is aware when a breakthrough will take place.
(c) A lot longer than one thinks a person can continue and hold on with hurting circumstances.
(d) The drowsy and dull eyes sparkled.
(e) There is surely a breakthrough for all of us.
(2) (a) hope (b) sparkled (c) impossible (d) breakthrough (e) restrictions

(B) (1) The most risky and dangerous thing a person can do is to make negative, destructive and irreversible decisions. Such decisions are taken when he is at his lowest, weighted down by overwhelming surrounding conditions.

(2) Only the Almighty who has created a person's destiny has the answer to the first question that arises in mind. The question is... When will a breakthrough take place?

(3) One can continue and hold the hurting circumstances a lot longer than one thinks, one can.

(4) One fails to understand what activates a ray of hope or from where it actually originates. When a person discovers hope, a completely new individual is born.

(5) A newer version of self will occur when we power beyond our set parameters and start to push beyond our limits, changing impossible into possible.

(C) (1) (a) perhaps (b) initiates (c) limits (d) marvel
(2) person, however, overcome, breakthrough, today, anyone, sparkled, understood, become
(3) (a) victory (b) emergence (c) totality (d) health (e) origin
(4) (a) betterment (b) activates (c) overwhelming (d) drowsy (e) restrictions (f) irreversible

(D) (1) "We witness our patients for several months, perhaps for a few years."
(2) What appears like an end never is unless we decide to bring the end.
(3) gerund: damaging
(4) obligation
(5) advice

(E) (1) A person who does not believe in himself fails to discover new and self-progressive things. In frustration, he takes dangerous decisions that are filled with negativity and destruction. Such decisions are irreversible. As soon as he finds new hope, he realizes that the new beginning has commenced. A newer version of self appears only after he powers over his set constraints. When he starts to push beyond his limits, the impossible becomes possible.

(2) The passage conveys to me that even if my efforts result in complete adversity and disappointment, I should continue believing in myself for the final breakthrough. The passage further teaches me that I should never lose hope for a better and happy future. If I haven't yet found that ray of hope over my failures and self-restrictions, I should keep on searching for it wisely and patiently. I must push above my set limits and never accept less than what I actually aim in life.

(F) Hope: A newer self

Negative, destructive and irreversible decisions that a person makes are very dangerous. This happens when he is at his lowest, weighted down by crushing surrounding conditions. Self-belief will help him for his betterment. Soon he will overcome all the obstacles and challenges to emerge victorious. Only the God who has created his destiny knows when a breakthrough will take place. He can endure bad situations way longer than he thinks. Hope is a phenomenon and thus, one fails to understand what activates a ray of hope or from where it actually originates. Hence, when a person discovers hope, a birth of a completely new individual takes place. As soon as one realizes that the fresh beginning has arrived, a new hope is found. However, a breakthrough is present for all but it totally depends on us. Probably, a newer version of self will not emerge until we excel beyond our limitations.

8. Samudragupta

(A) (1) False (2) True (3) False (4) False (5) True

(B) (1) emerged as an accomplished scholar.
(2) the age of fine art and learning.
(3) razor-sharp intelligence and military qualities as a warrior.
(4) holds a unique spot.
(5) poor, needy and helped the distressed.

(C) (1) (a) distinguished (b) musical (c) Samudragupta (d) contemporary (e) kingdoms

(2) (a) a person who comes after somebody else and takes his/her place
(b) an ability or a calibre
(c) caring and generous
(d) the head of the state; king
(e) a length of time in the life of a particular person in history

(3) (a) passage of time: Nothing is going to change between them with the <u>passage of time</u>.

(b) by the way: By the way, Ms. Deena will come to your house in a while to examine you.
(c) aware of the fact: I wasn't aware of the fact that she is visiting me today.
(d) diplomatic skills: Displaying false compassion is one of the many diplomatic skills of most of the politicians.
(e) attributed to him: The beautiful poem 'A Wedding Proposal' is attributed to him. *(a poem from the book 'Fragrance' by Firoz Tata)*

(4) (a) life, time (b) out, standing (c) beg, an (d) conquer, or (e) fat, her

(D) (1) (a) write – written (b) flourish – flourishing (c) consider – considering (d) attribute – attributed (e) administer – administered (f) play – playing

(2) (a) model: The architect had produced a small-scale model of the proposed shopping mall.
model: The beautiful model has dressed herself in a purple gown.
(b) veena: My Keny loves to play musical instrument, veena.
veena: Veena is my childhood friend.
(c) father: He is a loving and caring father to his adopted girl.
father: She visited the church for a confession to the holy father.

(3) This great Gupta king was a great conqueror and an outstanding diplomat.

(4) Samudragupta was greater than any other Gupta ruler.

(5) The king always worries about the need for educating his subjects.

(6) Present participle: They spent a lot of time in walking. Gerund: Walking is the best exercise for us.
Present participle: The boy was travelling to his native place. Gerund: Travelling is my favourite hobby.

(E) (1) Emperor Ashoka Maurya is regarded as one of the most prominent personalities in ancient Indian history. He inhabits a unique spot in the history of mankind. Although in 273 BCE, he succeeded his father Bindusara, he was crowned in 269 BCE due to internal wars. He was a man with multifaceted shades. With his efforts and patronage, Buddhism started to be transformed into a world religion. In his daily life he practiced accord, non-aggression and tolerance. He completely gave up the conquest through arms after his victory in the Kalinga war. His main idea was to promote unity among mankind under the dominion of the Dharma and the serenity of all men and animals. Ashoka possessed authentic and genuine qualities of heart and head, superb statesmanship and a military genius. He was a man of truthfulness, uprightness and sincerity. He is considered to be a flawless royal saint and a figure next to Lord Gautama Buddha. Despite his true religious spirit, he continued to be an imperialist. Gradually, the Buddhist enthusiasm of Ashoka resulted into the decay, disintegration and downfall of the Mauryans.

(2) According to me, a good king must exhibit certain important qualities that make him extremely famous and successful. He must be clear and concise at all times. He must possess important decision-making ability, must be courageous, passionate and dedicated for the welfare of his subjects. He must have humility and should work in the direction of his empire-building. He must be charitable by nature as well as compassionate towards the needs of poor and needy. He must always encourage his strategic thinking, staying ethical as well as civic-minded.

(3) It is our duty to see that historical sites are not in any sort of danger caused due to pollution, uncontrolled urbanization, tourism or irresponsible citizens. Whenever we visit the site we must keep the standards of hygiene and purity high. We must obey and follow the said guidelines by the authorities. We must also encourage others to do so.

(F) Samudragupta: The great Gupta ruler

Samudragupta, the successor of Chandragupta I is regarded as the greatest among all the Guptas. Dr. Vincent Smith regards him as the 'Napoleon of India'. His military conquests are known from *Prayag Prashati* written by Harisena, his court poet. The poet has described him as a kind and generous man. Gradually, he emerged as a talented scholar. He fought several battles and is considered as one of the unforgettable Gupta emperors whose period is famed as the age of fine art and learning. He possessed high intellect and military merits. He was a great scholar-poet who also learnt Vedas. He won the distant kingdoms by his policy of conciliation and pardoned those who submitted to him. He was kind to the poor and helped the distressed. He is also attributed for his influence in the progress of Indian culture. He was known for his liking for poetries and music, earning him the title of '*Kaviraja*'. A poetical work called '*Krishna Charitam*' is credited to him. His lyric coins show him playing a veena. According to many, the Golden Period of Indian ancient history began during his reign.

PPP

9. Visualization

(A) (1) (a) A person can visualize his/her life as he/she hopes and wants.
(b) As our feet touch the ground, we feel a sense of blessings and gratitude.
(c) Before going for a shower, feel calm, composed and easy.
(d) Exercise and/or meditation makes us feel fresh and energetic.
(e) After reaching home, one wants to sit down and relax.
(f) Life keeps messing up our plans.

(2) (a) discoverer (b) self-controlled (c) environment (d) see it

(B) (1) In the passage the writer has described morning with bright blue sky. The warm morning sunlight is entering through the slightly opened window of the room. The birds are pleasantly chirping on a fruit tree next to the window.

(2) As soon as feet touch the ground, one feels a sense of blessings and gratitude for having yet another day in life. In mind, a person must say that he/she is grateful, delighted and excited for the day.

(3) The writer suggests taking our own time and being patient while brushing teeth. He asks us to imagine as if we are brushing each tooth carefully. Further, one must be calm and relaxed while taking shower and select from the previous day what has to be worn the next day.

(4) According to the writer, we must encourage ourselves to motivate and uplift others, lead and guide them, share and learn things from others, patiently listen to them and stay progressive and unbiased towards others. We must respect the feelings, reactions and views of others.

(5) We must be grateful for whatever we have in life compared to several dismayed, distressed and destitute people. We must also be thankful for today and waking up tomorrow healthy, energized and refreshed. The main reason for being grateful is that life can mess up our plans at any moment and no one can guarantee what actually tomorrow may bring.

(C) (1) eyes, sunlight, birds, fruit, tree, window, tooth, home, bed
(2) idea, blessings, manner, danger, self-control, respect, truth

(D) (1) No sooner did I go to bed than I fell asleep.

(2) A viewpoint is provided by strong faith.
(3) He asked what kind of visualization I (the narrator) liked.
(4) She avoided engrossing into her creative thoughts until recently.
(5) What do you want to do?

(E) (1) I begin my day by remembering the name of the closest person to my heart. After brushing and showering, I spent some time praying. I visualize my day to be happy, healthy, productive and peaceful. As I love to write my mind on paper, I keep visualizing new creative notions and imaginations.

(2) Yes, I do agree. Until we do not learn to respect the feelings, reactions and views of others, they too won't make an attempt to understand ours. Making an effort to know and understand the emotional state and opinions of others is a mark of a progressive, matured and intelligent individual.

(3) Staying attentive and focused in life is crucial as it helps to reduce stress and provide freedom from tension. It even helps us to attain our set goals faster than usual and without much difficulty. Gradually, our understanding power increases with the practice of being attentive and focused.

(F) A visible form

Creation of mental visual images and the act or process of interpreting in visual terms or of putting into visible form is known as 'visualization'. When we imagine every step of an activity, our mind and body starts to get ready to take necessary steps in real life. Moreover, visualization allows us to remember and mentally practice our planned movements. Although it does not change our life, it surely changes how we approach and perceive it. Visualization can be achieved through a few mental preparations, creating images in mind, generating a visual picture along with an affirmation for each goal and using those affirmations to support visualization.

ÞÞÞ

10. Online Shopping: Advantages and Disadvantages

(A) (1) (a) agree (b) disagree (c) disagree (f) agree (e) disagree

(2) (a) the emergence of the World Wide Web.
(b) experience of shopping.
(c) compare prices from hundreds of different vendors.
(d) fraud and security threats.
(e) responsible, intelligent and experienced internet user and an online shopper.

(B) (1) Notionpress, Decathlon, Flipkart, eBay, Snapdeal and Amazon are some of the popular and trusted online shopping websites mentioned in the passage.

(2) Books, clothing, household appliances, toys, hardware, software, grocery, electronics, etc. are some of the hundreds of products consumers can buy from an online store.

(3) Slow online connectivity and devices infected by the viruses are some of the other online issues highlighted in the above passage.

(4) Shopping round the clock, time saving to search products, cheaper deals, better prices, discount coupons, return, exchange, refunds, reviews and photographs of the product helping to purchase confidently are some of the

advantages of online shopping mentioned in the passage.

(5) Sometimes online shoppers have to face fraud, security threats and attacks from the hacker. Some online stores are bogus and collect card and other security details of the customers. An online shopper cannot try or examine the things before buying. Sometimes, the product descriptions are cleverly created to present the product in more interesting and attractive manner. These are some of the disadvantages of online shopping mentioned in the passage.

(C) (1) i – v, ii – iv, iii – given extra, iv – ii, v – iii, vi – i

(2) (a) online: notionpress.com is my favourite online book store.
(b) hacker: A hacker is a person who secretly finds a way of looking at and/or altering information on somebody else's computer system without permission.
(c) customer: notionpress.com has an excellent customer service department.
(d) shoppers: Each day notionpress.com receive orders from hundreds of shoppers around the country.

(3) (a) enjoyment (b) effort (c) responsibility (d) intelligence

(D) (1) Time – Past Tense; Aspect – Progressive (continuous)
(2) Online shopping was done by the boy.
(3) The grandmother was being helped by Delzin.
(4) The photographs of the product from various angles helps to purchase the product confidently.
(5) (i) She is studying hard so that she can get a first class.
(ii) Put on your winter clothes lest you should catch a chill.
(iii) The WHO was formed in order that international public health standards around the globe would improve.

(E) (1) According to me, online shopping is much better, easy and convenient compared to old and traditional way of shopping. In case of online shopping, one can shop by sitting in comfort of home. Online shopping offers plentiful varieties for each and every product. We can even compare the cost of the products by browsing through different websites. Home delivery option reduces the stress to go out and wander in scorching sun for hours to buy things. Return and replace policies further add additional advantage in online shopping. This saves ample amount of time and energy to go back to the store and argue and/or convince the shopkeeper to return or replace the product. Sometimes discounts and money back offers make online shopping more irresistible.

(2) Yes, just last month for my younger sister's birthday I did online shopping of a remote control truck to gift her. My overall experience was very satisfying. I got an opportunity to choose from wide variety of toy trucks belonging to various brands. I selected cash on delivery option among other e-payment options. Just in three days the parcel got delivered at home. I received certain number of points after the purchase which I availed later for my next online purchase. Thus, my experience of online shopping was simply excellent.

(3) Meesho, Ajio, Myntra, ShopCules, Zivame, Limeroad, Wizbiker, Bumsonthesaddle, etc.

(F) The modern form of shopping

In today's time, shopping online is very common. Merchants sell various products on the internet. Shoppers can view online stores from their homes and shops through their devices. Numerous brand new products are sold and delivered daily through countless online sites. Cheaper online deals accompanied by better prices are easily and conveniently available. However, in the case of traditional way of shopping, one has to visit crowded places looking for the product until it is found. Several times, long queue for paying bills becomes a serious headache. Online shopping is not free from some of its drawbacks and disadvantages. Online fraud and security threats through hackers have become common. Occasionally, product descriptions are shrewdly created to make the product more presentable. Slow online connectivity, time zone differences and devices infected by the viruses are some of the other issues. One has to be a responsible, smart and skilled internet user and an online shopper.

ÞÞÞ

11. Motivation: The Master of Successful Life

(A) (1) motivation (2) obstacles (3) success (4) hopes

(B) (1) One can yield the fruits of sweet success by pushing the self beyond the normal capacities.

(2) The successful people do extra hard work that some of us do not.

(3) Based on the passage, the basic need of a human is to gain recognition, dignity, money, power, position and fame.

(4) In order to be successful, one needs high dedication, discipline and motivation. Motivation thrives an individual towards success.

(5) The road to success is described as hard, long, laborious, boring and tiresome. If we have motivation as our dependable buddy, then there is no need to worry about anything.

(6) A person may not always be rewarded with success since life may have some other hidden plans. A person has to fail many times before getting up again and again to move forward towards attaining success. Difficulties make us strong and worthy of success. Thus, we must always stay motivated to move ahead in life. In this way, the search for success is described in the passage.

(C) (1) (a) motivate (verb) (b) passionate (adjective) (c) perform (verb) (d) accomplish (verb) (e) positive (adjective)
(2) (a) passion (noun) (b) quickly (adverb) (c) positively (adverb) (d) performance (noun) (e) success (noun)
(3) (a) success (b) sweet (c) ahead (d) motivated (e) boring

(D) (1) A person may not always be rewarded with success while searching for it.
(2) Which one was accomplished quickly and with a better outcome?
(3) Failures will be unable to stop her.
(4) One needs nothing to be successful but high dedication, discipline and motivation.
(5) Life has been hitting you in the head.
(6) (i) You must have responded to such work neither passionately nor positively.
(ii) Even if you have started up, moved on and faced challenges, you still need to push it beyond what your normal capacities are, only then one can yield the fruits of sweet success.

(E) (1) Yes, according to me motivation is very necessary to succeed. It helps us to come out from negative thoughts and adverse conditions, striving us towards our goal. Moreover, it makes us more focused and assists us to overlook all the excuses that we give in our day-to-day life. When I see someone has achieved great success after overcoming odds, it motivates me the most. It gives me motivation that if others can accomplish their dreams through dedication and hardship, so can I.

(2) According to me, the line... *Life hits you in the head and one has to fall down many times before getting up and moving ahead* can be explained as... Many of us frequently face failures in life. It makes us feel dejected and thus, we perhaps

stop continuing towards our goal. However, the one who gathers the courage and stands up from the failures, has the potential to achieve long-lasting success. Life is full of obstacles and we are bound to encounter several hindrances and failures again and again in achieving our goals. However, the person who overcomes the failures and gets up from the beat down becomes stronger and more determined to never give up in pursuing the goals.

(3) From the above text I have learnt that motivation helps us to kick-off from where we have stopped. Once the person feels motivated and confident to achieve, he will keep paving towards the path of success. Life is full of obstacles and to overcome those obstacles first we need to prepare our own self mentally. We should not worry about our failures and always keep our hopes alive. Failures should be considered as each ladder of experience towards success. We should keep pushing and inspiring ourselves to attain countless feats in life.

(F) The road to success

Success is important to all as it helps us to gain recognition, dignity, money, power, position and fame. One needs to be highly dedicated, disciplined and motivated to be successful. It is human tendency to accomplish a task of choice faster with better results. However without motivation it is not possible. Starting something is the most challenging part of the task. With the help of motivation, once things get started, there is no turning back. In search of success, it is important for the individual to be mentally strong and prepared to face obstacles and different challenges. Therefore, staying motivated to keep pushing forward is essential. Successful people do extra hard work making them more successful. Pushing beyond the normal limits can produce the unimaginable fruits of sweet success. Only motivation can be our reliable friend on the road to success, which is full of hard, long, difficult, tedious and frustrating hurdles. Hence, keeping the hopes alive, drive yourself with motivation in search of a cheerful and prosperous tomorrow.

ppp

12. World Health Organization

(A) (1) researches in medical (2) 194 member states (3) 24th July 1948 (4) support to worldwide healthcare

(B) (1) The World Health Organization is mainly responsible for international public health and improving the health standards of the people around the globe.

(2) The main objective of WHO Constitution states the *attainment by all people of the highest possible level of health.*

(3) WHO headquarter is situated in Geneva, Switzerland. It has 6 semi-autonomous regional offices and 150 field offices from various nations.

(4) Every year, World Health Day is observed on 7th April.

(5) The World Health Report is the prominent publication of the World Health Organization. It provides expert assessments of global health topics and health statistics of all the nations.

(6) The World Health Organization has played a key role in numerous public health achievements, particularly the eradication of smallpox and polio as well as the development of an Ebola vaccine. Its present priorities not only include infectious diseases like tuberculosis, AIDS, Ebola and COVID-19, but also non-infectious diseases like heart disease and cancer.

(7) Tedros Adhanom Ghebreyesus is the current Director General of WHO. He belongs to the Ethiopian nationality.

(C) (1) (a) assessment (b) promoting (c) professional (d) sustainable
(2) (a) achievements (b) eradication (c) responsible (d) include (e) improving (f) majority

(D) (1) The Director General of WHO did not speak in favour of the idea.

(2) (a) **Blew:** The strong winds blew the dust into the sky.
Blue: The girl was wearing a blue top paired with denim jeans.
(b) **Brake:** The harder the brake pedal is pressed, the greater the car's deceleration.
Break: The dog bit the old man, but didn't break his skin.

(3) WHO serves as an opportunity for meetings and discussions on world health issues.

(4) A few organizations carry power but they are not very tactful.

(5) That is the best thing that has happened to me. Subordinate Adjective Clause

(E) (1) Just two lanes away we have a very well-known social organization called '*Nari Uddhar*'. This group works to improve the condition of distressed women. Recently, with the help of a local political leader the group has built a public toilet for women. Free sanitary napkins and basic medicines are also provided by them to the needy women in our vicinity. The organization makes sure that all the girls below the age of 14 receive free education. Employment opportunities for women are also created by them. Moreover, cases of domestic violence and women harassment are also registered and solved by them.

(2) The International Labour Organization is a United Nations agency whose duty is to develop social and economic fairness. It establishes international labour standards. The agency was founded in October 1919. The ILO has 187 member states and is headquartered in Geneva, Switzerland. The organization focuses on the workers' minimum wages, their working hours, housing and compensation after an accident. It works to improve the labour laws in the underdeveloped countries. Moreover, it frames model codes and safety guidelines for industries. International labour standards of ILO are mostly aimed at safeguarding productive and sustainable work worldwide in an environment of liberty, impartiality, safety and self-respect. ILO works hard to protect the freedom of association and the effective recognition of the right to collective bargaining, abolition of child labour, exclusion of discrimination in respect to employment and the abolition of forced or compulsory labour. Thus, ILO is successively a chief contributor to international labour laws. It also aims to provide technical aid to developing nations. In 2019, the agency summoned the Global Commission on the Future of Work, whose report made ten suggestions for governments to meet the challenges of the 21st century labour situation. These recommendations include a right to lifelong learning, universal labour assurance and social security from birth to old age.

(F) WHO: An agency of the UN

WHO, a dedicated agency of the United Nations was established on 7th April 1948. Every year the date is observed as World Health Day. The agency comprises representatives from 194 member states. It is not only accountable for improving the health standards of the people around the world but also organizes responses to health crises. It is headquartered in Geneva, Switzerland and has 6 semi-autonomous regional offices and 150 field offices from various nations. The organization also provides technical help to those countries that set international health standards. The World Health Report as its prominent publication provides expert assessments of global health topics and health statistics of all nations. The WHO has played an important role in several public health achievements. Eradication of smallpox and polio as well as the development of an Ebola vaccine are credited to WHO. Existing priorities of the agency not only include infectious diseases like tuberculosis, AIDS, Ebola and COVID-19, but also non-infectious diseases like heart disease and cancer. It also emphasises on healthy diet, nutrition and food security and substance abuse. The current Director General of WHO is Tedros Adhanom Ghebreyesus who was appointed to the position on 1st July 2017. Its total approved budget for 2020-2021 is over 7.2 billion dollars, of which the majority comes from voluntary aid.

ꝒꝒꝒ

13. Freedom over Troubles

(A) (1) Sentences (a), (b) and (d) are the false sentences. The correct sentences are... (a) The bear was given a special warm place to stay in the barn. (b) The bear climbed into the farmer's cart. (d) When summer came, the bear started to watch over the beehives and had a lick of honey now and then.

(2) (a) The bear said these words to himself after he tricked the farmer to run away in the forest for his freedom.
(b) The farmer said these words to the bear when he realized that the animal (bear) had no warm and cozy place to sleep in the winter.
(c) The bear said these words to the farmer when he met the farmer describing his problem.
(d) The bear said these words to the farmer when he stepped out of the barn's gates.
(e) The farmer said these words to the bear when he decided to take the bear with him to his house.

(B) (1) they slept through the season.

(2) licked honey now and then.

(3) The bear had an ample amount of fat under his skin on which he could feed himself easily all through the winter.

(4) Looking after the beehives in summer was the condition that the farmer kept before taking the bear to his house.

(5) The farmer and his wife took very good care of the bear. He was given a special comfortable warm place to stay and had enough to eat in the barn. When summer came, the bear even had a lick of honey now and then.

(6) The bear could not wander freely because of the thick iron chain he wore around his neck. The bear started to miss his freedom to roam anywhere.

(C) (1) wander, roam

(2) (a) shelter (b) farmer (c) honey (d) barn (e) cart

(3) (a) mouth-watering: something that looks and/or smells very good
The lovely South Indian cuisine prepared by our Deena appeared mouth-watering.
(b) lucky stars: something that brings good luck/fortune
He thanked his lucky stars for having such a wonderful wife.
(c) instantly: happening immediately or suddenly
He instantly regretted his decision.
(d) cozy: warm and comfortable
On cold Christmas night, Fillu and Deny felt warm and cozy sitting by the fireplace in their house.
(e) wander: to walk somewhere slowly with no particular purpose
You don't need to wander alone on the dark streets.

(D) (1) (i) We must drink at least eight glasses of water daily. (noun)
(ii) "Water the plant or it will die," said the gardener. (verb)
(2) The bear will focus on what to eat.
(3) The animal was very happy with his comfortable life.
(4) Until the summer arrived, he (the bear) had to do nothing in return.
(5) The farmer requested repeatedly to come.

(E) (1) We all love our individual freedom. I will firmly dislike if someone hinders my freedom while providing me with all the other luxuries and comforts of life. We all adore our respective freedoms and at the same time, we must respect the freedom of others too. Worldly comforts are worthless at the price of one's captivity and restrictions.

(2) (a) The line... I have nothing to protect myself from the cold and chilling winds besides this fur on my body, which is not enough. This line clearly shows that the bear is finding himself helpless and stranded against the cold. (b) The line... The animal was very pleased with his comfortable life, clearly indicating that the bear was happy.

(3) I completely disagree with encroaching on the freedom of birds by caging them for fun and past time. Just like us, every living thing on our planet has equal rights to live their lives freely and in peace. Even the birds must have the same rights to enjoy their freedom of movement.

(F) Freedom or cozy captivity?

The bear said to the farmer that he can survive without food and water in winter because he slept through the season. He had an ample amount of fat underneath his skin on which he could feed himself easily throughout the winter. However, besides inadequate fur on his body, the poor animal had nothing to protect himself from the cold and chilling winds. He was searching for a warm and cozy place to sleep. Hearing this, the farmer offered him a safe, warm and cozy place to live where the bear would be given enough food throughout the winter. Before taking the animal to his house, the farmer kept the condition that the bear would have to look after his beehives in summer. The bear agreed to the offer. Now he had a good comfy place to live and had enough to eat. When summer approached, he would look after the beehives and have a lick of honey. However, he missed his freedom of moving freely due to the thick iron chain around his neck. Finally, the bear got a chance to stretch himself by stepping out of the barn's gates. The bear thanked the couple and ran straight in the forest to enjoy his freedom.

14. Fossils

(A) (1) animals (2) waters (3) fossil (4) sedimentary (5) organism

(B) (1) Fossils are the remains of animals and plants that become hard over time and turn into rocks. The record confirms that most of the species present today are very different from the fossil species.

(2) Some of the important examples of fossils are wood replaced by minerals, bones preserved in tar pits, impressions of a leaf or stem in a rock, an insect trapped in firm and stiff plant sap and an animal trapped and frozen in the ice.

(3) Sedimentary rocks are types of rocks that are formed by the accumulation or deposition of mineral or organic particles at the earth's surface.

(4) Mud, sand and other fine particles at the bottom of the shallow seas are called 'sediments'.

(5) Most of the time, the hard parts of an organism such as a bone and/or tooth were preserved.

(6) The estimated time of the appearance of organisms can be determined by the position of their fossils in the layer of the rock.

(7) Most of the fossils were formed at the bottoms of the shallow seas. They are covered under a large part of the earth and slowly but surely, they are covered by sand and mud.

(C) (1) (a) pre-historic: connected with the time in history before information was written down
The first chapter of the book 'The Glorious History of Ancient India' authored by Firoz Tata explains that a period between the pre-historic and historic ages is regarded as a proto-historic period.
(b) frozen: extremely cold layer of ice
Firoz gazed at her, frozen with shock.
(c) imprint: to print or press a mark or design onto a surface
Our footprints imprint in the snow.
(d) appearance: the way that something or somebody looks on the outside
He had never been greatly concerned about his appearance.
(e) decayed: the process of being destroyed by natural causes
One of the old man's decayed teeth had dropped out.

(2) (a) remains (noun) (b) species (noun) (c) existing (adjective) (d) deposition (noun) (e) accumulation (adjective)

(3) pre-historic, substance, deposition, imprint

(D) (1) The organism decayed and its outline was left in the material that turned to rock. ***(or)*** The organism decayed making its outline in the material that turned to rock.
(2) How little we think about fossils until we read about them!
(3) Hadn't he read a book on fossils?
(4) I could possibly understand something more only if they had some of those incredible pictures of the fossils.
(5) (a) condition (b) request (c) suggestion (d) past ability

(E) (1) Soil formation is a long process. It is mainly made up of mineral particles, organic materials, air, water and living organisms. All of these materials interact gradually yet constantly. It takes millions of years because soil is formed by weathering of rocks, which is a very slow process. It takes many years to convert a huge piece of rock to small granules.

(F) Remains in the rocks

The fossils are a record of the animals and plants life that existed very long ago. They provide information about their remains that became hard over time and turned into the rocks. A fossil is an important piece of evidence from pre-historic times. Most of them are formed at the bottoms of the shallow seas. Sometimes, we find their imprint in the rock. They may have been completely covered. The outline of the organism is left in the material that turns into rock. Fossils are mostly found in the sedimentary rocks. Fossils discovered at the lower layers of rock are usually older than those discovered in the upper layers. The assessed time of the appearance of organisms can be determined by the position of their fossils in the layer of the rock. The ages of fossils can be determined according to the ages of the rocks where they were found.

15. Wisdom Hatched in a Proverb

(A) (1) (b) never be overenthusiastic and (d) not to expect highly favourable result before the actual outcome
(2) (a) be not so sure about something that is expected to happen in future and (c) wait until the good thing actually takes place
(3) (a) counting his chickens before they are hatched and (d) too enthusiastic and optimistic

(B) (1) The last sentence in the passage tells us that unnecessary and over enthusiasm towards something to take place can end in failure and discontentment.

(2) The girl in the passage was thinking about how many chicks she would have and how much money she would make by selling them. She was also thinking about the things she would buy in future with all that money.

(3) The writer advises those who purchase lottery tickets to hold their horses until the official announcement of the lottery comes out.

(4) Hold your horses, sometimes said as 'Hold the horses', means to wait or slow down. When someone says, hold your horses, it's a way of telling the other person to pause, hold on or stop for some time. The idiom is often used to tell someone to think about something before taking action.

(5) The writer has said that until the bud does not blossom into a beautiful flower, we cannot say that the bud will become a flower because it is possible that abruptly it can be plucked by someone.

(C) (1) enthusiasm
(2) (a) actually (b) reality (c) exactly (d) inevitability (e) likely (f) possibility
(3) (a) disappointment (b) proverb (c) hatch (d) announcement (e) dissatisfaction
(4) enthusiastic, optimistic, favourable
(5) In <u>reality</u>, it was not that easy to make the wrecked old house <u>beautiful</u> again.

(D) (1) Harshada was smarter than all the other girls in the class.
(2) No other girl in the class was as smart as Harshada.
(3) I was extremely moved when I recently read a very well explained proverb in one of the books of Firoz Tata titled 'Augmenting Your Knowledge'.
(4) The girl was attentive, so the teacher praised her.
(5) The girl in the purple skirt (subject), is (verb), is my friend (predicate)
(6) Does selling eggs worth two hundred rupees per week go far?
(7) While thinking about all this, she slipped and fell down.

(E) (1) A proverb is the fruit of wisdom of our ancestors. Yes, I completely agree with the wittiness of the proverb 'Do not count your chickens before they are hatched'. This proverb advises that it is silly to keep extremely high hopes on things that we do in our everyday life. One can surely dream big but to excel towards a desired dream, a person has to work hard to fulfil his longings. However, to be excessively ambitious or to plan beyond what reality permits may be unwise. A person should not count his chickens before they are hatched, and must understand that imaginary or anticipated things are not realities.

(2) 'Birds of a feather flock together' is a very popular and frequently used proverb. It is often found that birds of the same kind flock and fly together. For instance, a sparrow would not be seen flying together with a crow and vice versa. There are certain birds that flock together to cross the seas and oceans in search of warmer regions. Whenever

we see a flock of birds flying in the sky, we find that they all belong to the same class. Even people who are alike in nature or share similar kinds of habits accompany each other as they like to spend time together. Those who differ on viewpoints and outlooks, often find different paths in life. Hence, this proverb highlights the meaning of socializing and working in teamwork. A person's character can be determined by the company he keeps. If a person moves in a circle of drunkards, he will perhaps be the same. If he passes his time in the company of good men, his nature is likely to improve as he will learn several righteous values from them. Moreover, people with similar beliefs, culture, language, tastes, etc. often form groups and spend time with each other. Even countries keep friendly relations with the other countries having similar interests, goals and philosophies.

(F) Do not count your chickens before they are hatched

'Do not count your chickens before they are hatched' is a proverb that is used as a caution to someone to not plan anything in advance that depends on a thing which is likely to take place in the future. It guides us to hold ourselves until the good actually occurs. It teaches us not to be too sure about something that is anticipated to happen in future as it may never happen in reality. This proverb tries to save us from the regret and displeasure we may encounter in future. A person must not be too enthusiastic and optimistic about a favourable outcome of his choice. Therefore, until it becomes a reality, it is unwise to build too much hope on anything that we do. Too much enthusiasm for something to happen may end in disaster and displeasure.

16. Hey! It's Christmas Time

(A) (1) True (2) False (3) True (4) False (5) True

(B) (1) Colourful paper ribbons, flowers, balloons, wall streamers, small colourful electric bulbs, tiny pieces of decorative articles like dazzling plastic stars, balls, bells, fairies, mistletoe, candles, garlands, roping, swags, satin ribbons, poinsettias, wreaths, etc.

(2) Usually the Christmas tree is beautifully decorated with small colourful electric bulbs and other tiny pieces of decorative articles like dazzling plastic stars, balls, bells, fairies, mistletoe, etc.

(3) Santa Clause or Father Christmas appears to be a round bodied slightly fat man who stays happy and jolly. He has a white long beard and often wears eyeglasses. He dresses in a red coat with white fur collar. He wears a white fur-cuffed red trousers, red hat with white fur along with black leather belt and boots.

(4) Christmas pudding and plum cakes

(5) religions: Christians, Hindus and Muslims; festivals: Christmas, Diwali and Eid.

(C) (1) Lord, the son of God
(2) ecstatic
(3) (a) attract (b) exchange (c) ecstatic (d) son (e) adding (f) birth
(4) (a) astounding (b) a great day (c) religious belief (d) most popular (e) in their own ways (f) garlands

(D) (1) This day is celebrated with great splendour and joy, isn't it?
(2) No other day is as great as this day for the children.
(3) On Christmas, we <u>hate</u> to dress in <u>old</u> and <u>dull</u> clothes.
(4) Hadn't the family celebrated Christmas many times?

(5) It was ordered to surprise my darling Deena. (by me)

(E) (1) As Christmas being my most favourite festival, I try my best to make this auspicious day very special and enjoyable. Before a few days of the festival, I start to decorate my room, especially my enchanting Christmas tree. We buy new clothes and a few new items like crockery, curtains, bedsheets, etc. for our house. I write a letter to my dearest Santa Claus to express my gratitude for always bestowing his blessings on my family. On Christmas eve, I sleep in joyful anticipation to see my Christmas present the next morning. On Christmas, we visit a local organization for orphan children. We distribute candies, cakes and gifts among them. In the evening, we have a family get-together and relish a delicious dinner.

(2) If I ran short of money to buy a Christmas gift for my sibling, I would request and borrow from someone else close to me. For instance, if I wanted to buy a word scrabble game for my younger sister and fell short of money, I would ask my mother to lend it to me. If I wanted to buy something for my mother and did not have the money for it, I would borrow from my father.

(3) Yes, I would certainly prefer visiting poor and needy children on the day of Christmas to distribute gifts and sweets among them. Christmas is a celebration of joy and spreading care and affection. We must feel blessed in bringing smiles on the faces of innocent children. For me, Christmas is not about receiving but surely about giving. The happiness that we put out has always its way of returning back to us.

(F) 25th December

Christmas, celebrated on 25th December is an annual festival honouring the birth of Lord Jesus Christ. It is celebrated by billions of people around the world. The day is celebrated with great splendour and joy. People love to dress in new colourful clothes. They wish 'Merry Christmas' to their friends, relatives and beloved ones. They visit one another's house to greet and exchange good wishes. Christmas cards, gifts, chocolates, cakes and sweets are sent and received. Whether rich or poor, young or old; all celebrate Christmas in their unique ways. The Christmas tree is decorated with different kinds of decorative ornaments. The tree looks amazing, adding a typical merry mood to the occasion. Delicious cuisines like Christmas pudding and plum cakes are prepared. Children sing Christmas carols in chorus to remember their Lord's birth. They eagerly look for gifts from their dear Santa. Christmas is also celebrated by many non-Christians.

17. A Fresh Beginning

(A) (1) (a) wild, malicious, wicked and jealous
(b) unintended, unknown and unfriendly
(c) a strange, mystical and miraculous life strength, which decided to test the death
(d) like the seed even we can create our path against all the impossible challenges
(e) the previous end

(2) (a) The seed got swollen with confidence and determination.
(b) There is the power to turn ends into transformations.
(c) The dying heart of the confined kernel cried out.
(d) The wicked wind abducted the little seed.

(B) (1) An innocent family of little kernels lived happily. Without an invitation, wild and malicious wind invaded them.

(2) The wicked wind abducted one of the defenceless little seeds. It carried away the seed until it grew weary and fed up with its entire adventure.

(3) The wild wind dragged the little kernel onto a strange and alien seashore.

(4) The first gentle drop of morning mist oozed into the crack.

(5) The seed happily greeted the cool pleasant moisture.

(6) From the last paragraph of the passage, I learn that if the tiny seed can face so many challenges and come out victorious we humans too can. A new beginning awaits on the other side of every end. The end that we see may be just a small pause before the birth of a fresh vision and a new occasion. I further learn that in us we have the power to turn ends into changes. Just as the 'once helpless seed' led its way through the concrete, we too can break through into a new and delightful life.

(C) (1) wild, malicious, peaceful, innocent, little, wicked, defenceless, weary, fed up, entire
(2) little kernel, little fellow, little one, poor fellow, tiny fellow
(3) under, stand, and, sand, rest, test, sad, tear

(D) (1) gerund: learning
sentence: Deena is a woman of great learning.
(2) dropping, dropped; breaking, broken
(3) Who will win the battle?
(4) The seed said that there it came, paving its path against impossible odds.
(5) How happy the little seed was!

(E) (1) Some of the qualities that I noticed in the little seed were its innocence, determination, optimism and strength to endure and overcome the difficult situation. My best quality is to never give up and struggle until I succeed. How hard and difficult things turn out to be, I never give up on my hope and I do not like to quit. Without stopping, I work to succeed and try harder to accomplish my goal.

(2) Yes, I do find correlation between our and the life of the little seed. Strong-minded and determined people who succeed in life never give up on their hopes and dreams in front of failures and disappointments. They embrace failures, work harder and rise again. Although the little seed was brutally separated from its family, it stayed strong and hopeful by not giving up its hope and dream of beginning a new life.

(F) A new start

Wild, malicious and wicked wind captured a little seed and carried it away until it got tired and weak. The rough wind dragged the little seed onto a bizarre and unfamiliar seashore. The seed kept rolling across a concrete pavement until it was stopped by a dry crack in the barren cement. Soon a heel of a leather boot stepped on it. The seed was jammed deep in the crack. The lost fellow decided to test the death as it wanted to stay alive. The seed happily absorbed the cool pleasant moisture. Soon little wisps of dust slipped into the crack. Silently tiny hairy roots were born with the help of more moisture and nourishment. The seed was born with a new life, breaking wide open. Thus, every end leads to a new beginning. What may appear like an end may be the opening of a new awaited opportunity. We have the power to turn ends into alterations.

18. The Brain

(A) (1) (a) agree (b) disagree (c) disagree (d) disagree (e) agree
(2) (a) cerebrum (b) brain (c) cerebrum (d) medulla (e) cerebellum

(B) (1) The writer in the passage has made the use of the word 'matter' in context of the soft tissues of the brain that includes grey and white matter. He further says that this matter contains the nerve cells, small blood vessels and non-neuronal cells that helps to maintain neurons and brain health.

(2) The human brain is divided into three major parts. They are cerebrum, cerebellum and medulla.

(3) The Cerebrum determines the intelligence of an individual. Thinking and alertness of a person actually origins from cerebrum. It also regulates person's memory, learning and some of the body's voluntary movements. Even hearing, seeing, touching, tasting and smelling abilities are controlled by cerebrum.

(4) The cerebellum, a major structure of the hindbrain is located near the brainstem behind and below the cerebrum.

(5) Cerebellum's major role is to maintain the balanced senses of the body, helping in coordinating voluntary movements. Thus, it is responsible for a number of roles including muscular activities like walking, cycling, running and swimming as well as motor skills such as balance and posture.

(6) The medulla is located at the base of the skull, just below the cerebellum. It is connected with the spinal cord.

(7) The medulla controls the heartbeat, breathing rate, muscular action of the digestive tract and the secretion of certain glands.

(C) (1) i – vi, ii – iii, iii – i, iv – v, v – ii

(2) (a) brain: an organ inside the head that controls one's movements, thoughts, memory and feelings
Dr. Dang has a unique device to examine <u>brain</u> activity during sleep.
(b) spinal cord: the mass of nerves inside the spine that connects all parts of the body to the brain
Abruptly seeing him standing in front of her, a shiver ran down her <u>spinal cord</u>.
(c) skull: the bone structure that forms the head and protects and surrounds the brain
Her <u>skull</u> was overflowing with too many sad thoughts.
(d) brainstem: the central part of the brain that continues downwards to form the spinal cord
His car injury had damaged his <u>brainstem</u>.
(e) glands: an organ in a person's or an animal's body that produces a substance for the body to use
Her immune system <u>glands</u> are enlarged.
(f) coordinate: to organize the different parts of an activity
Deny was appointed as a new head administrator to <u>coordinate</u> the work of the hospital.

(3) cycling, running, swimming

(4) largely, highly, automatically

(5) brain, nervous system, nerve cells, soft tissues, blood vessels, cells, neurons, cerebrum, cerebellum, medulla, head, brainstem, motor skills, muscle, skull, spinal cord, heartbeat, breathing, digestive tract, glands, nerve fibres

(D) (1) with

(2) (a) assertive (b) interrogative (c) exclamatory (d) imperative (e) interrogative (f) assertive (g) exclamatory (h) imperative

(3) He had somehow understood.

(4) (a) decides – finite; to visit – non-finite

(b) continued – finite; to study – non-finite

(c) request – finite; to answer – non-finite

(d) have come – finite; to ask, to answer – non-finite

(5) all, the

(E) (1) Yes, I have read a book on the science of the human body titled 'Human Body Encyclopedia'. Some of the most interesting facts that I came across in the book were (i) the human nose is so sensitive that it can tell the difference between about 10,000 different aromas. (ii) our body's tiniest joint is on the smallest bone called stirrup which is deep inside the ear.

(2) According to me the qualities/skills needed to become a good brain surgeon are good hand-eye coordination, excellent vision as well as a blend of confidence and caution. Moreover, a good organisational ability and outstanding communication skills are needed. Even physical stamina to cope with long hours and the demanding nature of the work under intense pressure and stress are vital. Most importantly, a thorough knowledge of human anatomy and microsurgery techniques are crucial.

(F) The central organ of the human

As a major controller of our body, the brain is the chief organ of the human nervous system. It possesses about ten billion nerve cells. It is made of soft tissues that includes grey and white matter. The organ has a high water content and almost 60% of fat. Cerebrum, cerebellum and medulla are its three major parts. The cerebrum is the largest part that determines the intelligence of an individual. It also regulates memory, learning, some of our voluntary movements, hearing, seeing, touching, tasting and smelling. The cerebellum is much smaller and lies behind and below the cerebrum. Its major function is to maintain the balanced senses of the body. It is also responsible for a number of functions including motor skills such as balance and posture. The medulla is the smallest part of the brain connected with the spinal cord. It regulates heartbeat, breathing, muscular action of the digestive tract, the secretions of glands and certain reflexes like sneezing, coughing, vomiting and swallowing. All nerve fibers connecting the brain and spinal cord pass through the medulla.

PPP

19. The Animal Kingdom

(A) (1) biggest animal on the planet

(2) approximately 33 elephants

(3) owls to use them while preying at nights

(4) two categories in which animals are classified

(5) learn the behaviour of animals

(B) (1) Among animals, the various ways of having babies include giving birth to the young ones, while others, such as birds and reptiles like crocodiles and tortoises lay eggs from which the young ones hatch.

(2) Animals are classified into two categories of vertebrate and invertebrate.

(3) The Kitti's hog-nosed bat is regarded as the world's smallest mammal. It measures at 1.1 inches.

(4) Animals that have backbones running down the backs of their body are considered as vertebrates. Birds, reptiles, amphibians, fish and mammals are all vertebrates.

(5) Animals that do not have backbones in their body are considered invertebrates. A snail is an invertebrate. Jellyfish that live in water are yet another example of invertebrates.

(6) A habitat is made up of a group of plants and animals. Mountains, seas and forests are some of the important examples of many different types of natural habitats. The sea is regarded as the world's biggest habitat.

(7) A food chain is a series of living creatures in which each type of creature feeds on the one below it in the series. Insects are fairly lower down the food chain. Animals depend on one another for their food. Some animals eat plants and grass, while others hunt the plant-eater animals. Each food chain begins with plants.

(8) Animals that only eat plants are called herbivorous animals. Because of their plant diet, herbivorous animals typically have mouthparts adapted to crushing or grinding. Cows, goats, tortoises, horses, gorillas, deer, elephants, etc. are some of the examples of herbivorous animals. However, animals like wolves, lions, leopards, hyenas, polar bears, cheetahs, etc. are carnivorous animals. They hunt other grazing animals. Thus, a carnivore is an organism that mostly eats meat or the flesh of animals. Sometimes carnivores are called 'predators'.

(C) (1) elephants, goats, cows, crocodiles, tortoises, horses, gorillas, deer, polar bears, cheetahs

(2) (a) antarctic (b) elephant (c) herbivorous (d) invertebrate (e) amphibian

(3) adjectives: different, enormous, natural, wobbly, soft
nouns: colour, example, habitat, behaviour, animal
(i) different: Deena is too <u>different</u> compared to the other women of her age.
(ii) colour: Purple is my most favourite <u>colour</u>.
(iii) enormous: The problem faced by the political leader was <u>enormous</u>.
(iv) example: This is the best <u>example</u> of what happens when you lie to your parents.
(v) habitat: Volcanic eruption gradually led to the destruction of wildlife <u>habitat</u>.
(vi) natural: She was the <u>natural</u> choice for the job.
(vii) behaviour: The <u>behaviour</u> of the mischievous Firoz changed as soon as he saw his father.
(viii) wobbly: The morning got off to a <u>wobbly</u> start.
(ix) soft: The lush green grass was <u>soft</u> and springy.
(x) animal: Cat is my favourite pet <u>animal</u>.

(4) howl, roar

(D) (1) some
(2) A few animals are like tiny spots of dust.
(3) They can even survive without water.
(4) You have never seen an Antarctic blue whale.
(5) (c) They not only move to find food but also to save themselves from being killed.

(E) (1) Recently, I had an opportunity to visit a forest. One day my father's best friend Mr. Shambhu who works as a forest officer took me along into the forest. I was thrilled to experience for myself what my father had always spoken about the forest. The moment I entered the forest, a cover of darkness appeared in front of my eyes. The sky had almost vanished due to the canopy of leaves high above us. Dense vegetation had grown in all the directions and the air was somewhat wet, having a strange smell to it. We could clearly hear the sounds of insects, birds, animals and numerous other creatures. Although we could not see them, except for a few birds, we knew they were somewhere around. Different sounds echoed all over, making the forest scary and bizarre. I had no idea how Mr. Shambhu could find his way through the dense forest. I realized that easily an inexperienced person could get lost in the forest. Carefully we walked along with a lot of effort. The most painful thing about being in the forest were the mosquitoes. In spite of wearing high boots and fully covered clothes, they were managing to bite me. For the first time I saw some of my favourite animals from a short distance. I also saw diverse insects, birds, snakes, giant spiders, huge and tall trees, flowers and creepers. The experience was unforgettable. I was awestruck by the splendid creations of God and enthralled to see the beauty of nature so closely. Although it was an exciting experience, I would prefer to remain outside the forest.

(2) My favourite domestic animal is an elephant. It is a friendly animal, having beautiful eyes and a strong-long trunk. The spectacle of an elephant scattering water on its back with the help of its trunk is spectacular. It has a unique style of eating food with the help of its trunk. One could even take a ride on it. Its large floppy ears look magnificent. The royal walk of an elephant gives me a feeling of an approaching king displaying his confidence and valour.

(F) Animals

There are more than 1.5 million different types of animals on Earth, surviving in different kinds of conditions and places. They behave in different ways from one another. Some are as small as tiny dust spots. All animals breathe, feed and grow in their unique ways. As they have senses, they can see, hear, smell, taste, touch, hunt and defend themselves. Animals move to find food, to survive. They have various ways of having babies. Some give birth to their young ones. Birds and reptiles lay eggs. Vertebrate animals have backbones while the invertebrates do not. The skeleton supports their body and the muscles are used to move. Animal's certain behaviours have to be learnt by observing them. The place where an animal lives is called its habitat, which is made up of a group of plants and animals. As forests are full of trees, they offer animals a lot of space to make a home and plenty of food to eat. A food chain is a series of living creatures in which each type of creature feeds on the one below it in the series. All animals depend on other living things for food. Some animals eat plants and grass, while others hunt the plant-eaters. Animals that only eat plants are called herbivorous, while carnivorous animals hunt other grazing animals.

20. The Kindness Always Returns

(A) (1) Sentences (c) and (d) are the false sentences. The correct sentences are... (c) The three fat dwarfs in torn worn-out clothes and bare feet jumped in through the broken window (d) The clothes were so well made that the King, his Queen and several royal people loved to buy them.

(2) (a) The father (bootmaker) said these words to his daughter.
(b) The daughter said these words to her father.
(c) The father (bootmaker) said these words to his daughter.

(3) (a) The next morning, he went to his belongings to start the work.
(b) One bright moonlit night both decided to hide themselves in the house.
(c) Three fat dwarfs jumped in through the broken window.
(d) The little mallets beat *thapak-thak, thapak-thak*!
(e) The father decided to make a few pairs of boots for the tiny helpers.

(f) "Thank you dear little angels".
(g) The dwarfs jumped out of the window and vanished in the dark.
(h) Good fortune seemed always to be on the side of the father and daughter.

(B) (1) For many days, four pairs of new, beautiful shining boots all ready to sell were made and found near the belongings of the bootmaker.

(2) When the clock struck 12, three fat dwarfs in torn worn-out clothes and bare feet jumped in through the broken window. Hopping, singing and dancing they went up to the bootmaker's table and began their magical work with the leather.

(3) The needles of the three dwarfs magically flew fast back and forth. Their little mallets beat *thapak-thak, thapak-thak*! Before the bootmaker and his daughter could think of anything, leather boots were already made.

(4) The next morning, the father and his daughter decided to stitch some colourful clothes and a few pairs of leather boots for the three dwarfs as a token of their appreciation.

(5) The line, '*They happily slipped into their gifts*' means that the dwarfs joyfully wore the new small colourful clothes and tiny shiny boots that were put on the table as a token of appreciation by the bootmaker and his daughter.

(C) (1) kind men, tiny helpers, gentle souls, little angels, little chaps
(2) fat, dear, tiny, gentle, little
(3) hopping, singing, dancing, happily slipped into their gifts
(4) vanished

(D) (1) The dwarfs understood that their job was done. They jumped out of the window.
(2) Who spent a happy time stitching clothes and making boots?
(3) The daughter said that they should do something for those three dear dwarfs.
(4) His boots were so well made that the King, his Queen and several royal people loved to buy them.

(E) (1) Just like the father and his daughter, even I would have expressed my gratitude towards the dwarfs in my own way if they had helped me. I would have arranged for new clothes and shoes for them. Moreover, I would have also kept something delicious to eat and drink for the little men.

(F) The kind-hearted dwarfs

The bootmaker was again surprised to see four pairs of new, beautiful shining boots on his table. They were ready to be sold. Soon he became rich. As he wanted to find out who was making the boots for him, one night he and his daughter decided to see. At midnight, three fat dwarfs in torn worn-out clothes and bare feet jumped in their house through the window. They happily sat down and began their magical work. Before the father-daughter duo could think anything, new shining boots were already made. The next morning the daughter decided to stitch new clothes for them. The father made a few pairs of tiny boots for the tiny helpers. The following night the dwarfs were more than happy to see their gifts on the table. They understood that their job was done and so jumped out of the window and disappeared in the dark.

Printed by Libri Plureos GmbH in Hamburg,
Germany